LINDS!

Have adored you since the very first BOBBAY!!!

Thanks for supporting this book - very glad we've stayed connected all these years.

Happy Reading!

:)

THIS
IS
NOW
YOUR
COMPANY

By Mike Rognlien

ISBN 13: 978-1-63489-117-2

eISBN: 978-1-63489-118-9

Library of Congress Catalog Number: 2018935095

Printed in the United States of America

First Printing: 2018

22 21 20 19 18   5 4 3 2 1

Cover and interior design by Emily Rodvold

Wise Ink Creative Publishing

837 Glenwood Avenue

wiseinkpub.com

To order, visit itascabooks.com or call 1-800-901-3480. Reseller discounts available.

For my mom and dad, all of my incredible teachers, and all of the people who, like me, march to a slightly different drumbeat.

And, of course, Oprah.

TABLE OF

CONTENTS

PART THREE:
YOU AND . . . WELL, YOU

"This isn't a book. It is an in-your-face conversation between you and one of the most insightful, effective, and genuine pros in the field of human performance. Unlike so many in my professio, Mike's doesn't just write about creating a great organization–he has done it. I've seen first hand how his no-nonsense, credible, and conversational approach to personal and organizational change has helped Facebook become what it is today. Get ready for a conversation that will guide you to greatness."

Joseph Grenny, NYT-bestselling coauthor of
Crucial Conversations* and *Influencer

+ + +

"Don't let Mike Rognlien's spicy language fool you. He is as devoted as I am to the idea of leaders caring about their people, supporting their growth and development, and setting them up for success. His chapters on the fifty-fifty relationship between people and their managers and on giving and receiving feedback are worth the price of the book alone. Read *This Is Now Your Company*. You'll learn a lot and be thoroughly entertained in the process."

Ken Blanchard, coauthor of *The New One Minute*
Manager* and coeditor of *Servant Leadership in Action

FOREWORD

Facebook is a radically different place to work. A place that will change the world of work in the same way that Facebook, as a product, has changed all of our worlds. What makes Facebook different is not just the hacker culture, the move-fast-break-things spirit, the high-tech wizardry, or even the leadership prowess of CEO Mark Zuckerberg and COO Sheryl Sandberg. What makes Facebook different is how it's cultivated a radical idea: namely, that each human being is unique, and this uniqueness is a feature to be maximized. This is the very building block upon which the entire company is built.

Most companies do not see this uniqueness as a building block–in fact, they see it as a frailty, a bug to be fixed. Certainly not a feature. But Facebook's entire company is built on the single premise that one size fits one. That no two engineers are the same, that each salesperson is motivated by different things, that each designer is idiosyncratic, and that each leader must find his or her own way to individualize.

So while every other company is building standardized competency models for each role, against which every individual in that role will be judged and measured, their gaps identified, their weaknesses "fixed," Facebook is doing the opposite. It's helping each person to identify, claim, and contribute their unique strengths to the team. Because it seems to know that in every hallway, every meeting, and every conversation, the ingredients of excellence are as varied as the human race.

Mike not only embodies this sort of intelligent individualization; he also taught it to thousands and thousands of new Facebookers. If you worked at Facebook at any point during his six and a half years at the company, one of the first things you likely did was go through his talk on cultural ownership–The Call to Action–in "n00b orientation." It was in this talk that you learned a bit more about your personal connection to Facebook's mission, maybe some of Mark and Sheryl's practices, and a lot about your responsibilities to your colleagues. But also, here is where you learned about Facebook's radical strengths-based philosophy. Here is where you learned to take yourself seriously. Here is where you learned to identify what is unique about you and how to contribute your uniqueness to your team. Here is where you learned that this, at heart, is what Facebook would always ask of you. Mike and his team brought this all to life, for thousands of Facebookers, and showed each one of them how to make their unique dent in the world.

If Facebook has a unique culture, and if Facebook stands as an example of a better way to build a company–and it does–then Mike's insights, lessons, and passion helped make it so.

So if you want your company or your team to get as much from its people as Facebook does–as much collaboration, creativity, drive, resilience, "hackerness"–then read this book. It's a tell-all about what's really worth telling about Facebook.

Marcus Buckingham, NYT-bestselling coauthor of
First, Break All the Rules and author of
Now, Discover Your Strengths

PART ONE
YOU AND YOUR COMPANY

1 | The Chapter about What It's Really Like to Work at Facebook

www.facebook.com/careers

2 | The Chapter about the Rest of the Chapters

(Sorry if chapter 1 pissed you off, but this isn't going to be *that* kind of book.)

I first spoke about my work at Facebook at an external conference in late 2011. I had only been at the company for six short months and, I have to say, I was incredibly excited to be a featured speaker at a conference I had enjoyed in the past as an audience member.

For my breakout session about developing people at Facebook, I was assigned one of the myriad midsize breakout rooms. This, despite telling the conference organizers that every time my coworkers spoke externally, the events were standing-room only, even in really large spaces. I explained: "Hey, this is not my ego speaking, but I work at one of the most curiosity-inspiring organizations in the world right now. As soon as people see the word 'Facebook,' they will want to attend."

I wasn't wrong; they did show up, and in droves. The room was filled to overflowing—so much so that the facilities manager for the hotel came into the room and broke up my session before it even started, asking more than half the people in the room to please go find another talk. (I don't know if the now-commonplace "Yaaaaaaasssss!" was a thing at that time, but if it was, it was probably at least hovering in my thought bubble.)

I think I did an OK job with that session after the excitement of having my party busted up by the cops (all right, the hotel cops) subsided. While most people listened attentively as I spoke about Facebook's culture and philosophy, I could see that more than a few of them didn't really take me seriously. I'm not sure why they were there—maybe they hoped they'd get some free Facebook swag (they didn't) or some gossip on the company or its employees (they *certainly* didn't). It was clear to me that when I spoke about treating everyone in the company as a leader and expecting them to behave accordingly, it was to many in the audience an amusement at best and a totally idiotic way to completely fuck up a young company at worst. Their folded arms and their *Yeah, right!* body language spoke volumes.

(Quick side note here: yes, I used the F-word! Because it's what I used at the time and is biographically accurate! And yes, I know I used it in a "business" book. I could have opted to say "f*ck" instead, sure. And nobody, including you, would have thought that I meant "fack" or "fick" or "feck" or "flowers . . ." I'm trusting that you are capable of seeing that word and not losing it, and if you hate that word, don't read it out loud. Don't say it yourself. But it is a word people use, it's a word I occasionally use, and even if you don't, I hope we'll still be cool.)

"So you just let everyone in the company give the CEO feedback?" asked one woman, with thinly veiled snark. She was asking this in reference to my sharing that Mark

Zuckerberg, our CEO, did a full-company Q and A *every single Friday* at four o'clock, and anyone on the payroll could ask him a question, share feedback, challenge a decision, etc. And they did. (And no—I won't be talking about any of their questions or his answers. Again, not that kind of book.)

In every question from this doubting audience, there seemed to be an underlying disbelief that anything but the oldest of old school organizations would ever survive, let alone succeed. Feedback was always top-down or something you shouted on your way out the door as you lit the bridge between yourself and your former employer on fire. Big, risky ideas were great, but only after they were fully vetted and approved by someone much higher up on the org chart, and they certainly weren't something you could just let people take action on without any supervision or guidance or accountability. Authenticity—being who you really were at work?

HAHAHAHAHNOWAYHELLNONOTGOINGTOHAPPEN.

You get the idea. They weren't on board.

As I was putting away my laptop at the end of my session, a gentleman from a large and wealthy defense contractor came up to me with an *Awww, you and your ideas are adorable, son!* look on his face. He told me straight up that while I seemed smart and he'd enjoyed the talk, Facebook would never amount to anything and I should enjoy the ride while I could.

K.

Even though it was clear to me in those early days that

Facebook was going to become something much bigger than it was when I joined, it wasn't a sure thing. And that first conference was a harbinger; over the next couple of years, I had lots of those experiences with people in my field (HR and Learning & Development, specifically), who doubted—openly and often loudly—that what we were building would work. Not all of the things we built *did* work. But Facebook didn't become the juggernaut it is today because we *didn't* try a hell of a lot of risky things that other people and their organizations laughed at.

As time went by, more audiences came into my life and I into theirs. I spoke at conferences, I spoke in our orientations, I taught tons of classes, and I hosted lots of visiting executives and teams whose businesses advertised on Facebook. I built manager training—training on handling difficulty, confrontation, and bias and digging deep into yourself to figure out who you really are and how to be just that. Without exception, every one of the groups that sat and listened to what I had to say felt that we at least had something worth learning a bit about. After all, we had free ice cream and some employees wore denim, and the place didn't collapse to utter shit as a result.

Much to my delight, it became a fairly significant part of my job to tell the Facebook story, but more importantly, to help other people see themselves in that story. And to inspire them to create their own.

This book isn't a juicy or dramatic retelling of that story. I find no value in any type of a "tell-all" book—first and foremost, because "all" is not "all" at all. The telling is usually done by people who have a bone they feel is best picked in the pages of a book. I have no such bones to pick—quite the opposite. Facebook grew from 1,700 to 25,000 employees in the time I worked there, and it was the most exhilarating, heart-filling, difficult, and draining work I've ever done. At the end of my time there I was filled with nothing but gratitude. But my memoirs of that time aren't terribly interesting to most people who aren't me.

What I think *is* interesting, and what prompted me to write this book, is the running list of things I've spoken about, taught, and learned/unlearned/relearned in my career. And not just at Facebook, but over the course of fifteen years of working in learning and development and being an active member of the cultural makeup of every company that has ever employed me. It is that list of topics and experiences—things I was known for at Facebook, I think, but also throughout my career—that might be valuable to you.

I *can* say that I recommend working at Facebook or a company like Facebook 110,000 percent. When Sheryl Sandberg, Facebook's brilliant COO and someone I will forever cherish working with, was deciding whether to take her job at Google, Eric Schmidt said to her: "When someone offers you a seat on a rocket ship, you don't ask which seat. You get on."

Amen, Eric Schmidt.

I want everyone on this planet to find their rocket ship. Or to create it. The content in this book speaks to some of the most valuable stuff I've done in my career, stuff that can help you make it to your rocket ship. I've seen my fair share of people who seemingly had all the right stuff on paper only to fail when it came time to get things done. And I've seen some really brilliant assholes—people who were among the best in their fields but insufferable to work with.

But, most importantly, I've seen a lot of amazing people do some incredible things, and there are some skills, beliefs, and attributes—ironically, most of them labeled "soft skills" despite being the hardest to master—that I think are common among them.

My job is to help you figure out how to apply those very skills and attributes in a way that will serve you well along the way. If you want one of the particular seats on the rocket ship that says "Culture Badass," I have a few ideas.

All of this speaks to a core belief I hold dear: any and every company can be a rocket ship if the crew works at it tirelessly. You are one of those crew members, no matter what you've been told in the past.

But you shouldn't feel compelled to build "the Facebook of banking." Or of construction. Or of anything. My favorite visitors to Facebook were the ones who came from organizations that looked and created things and acted *nothing* like Facebook. It was from one of them—a CEO of a bank, if I recall correctly—that I learned that the thing a company needed to do to be a great place for its employees to work was NOT to copy Facebook; any organization can be the best place on the planet (or the best rocket ship in the solar system) if the people who work there believe it can be and are crystal clear about who they are and what they value. They also need to work relentlessly to the highest of standards—not only in terms of how they behave but also, more importantly, how they hold themselves and others *accountable* for how they behave.

There are people out there—you may be one of them—who wake up every morning and can't wait to put on a suit and tie and get to their desks at exactly nine o'clock sharp so that they can build beautiful spreadsheets and make up lots of rules and regulations that someone else can enforce. If the people who run their organizations figure out what matters most to these weirdos (I kid—fly that flag, actuarial overlord!), I believe they'll win.

So how do we get there?

Since I'm a trainer by trade, I've broken up things in this book to make them more learnable and digestable in whatever-sized bites you're up to taking as you're reading it. The three sections of this book are divided mostly by the applicability of the skills in question. There's a section that focuses primarily—not exclusively—on you and the way you engage with your company and its culture. There's a section that focuses primarily—not exclusively—on how you engage with the people you work with, like your manager or your peers. And, finally, the largest and last section of the book is—exclusively—all about you.

Regardless of the section, though, every chapter in this book represents a skill or practice or philosophy that I have seen really awesome people (sometimes, when I'm at my best, me!) use in great organizations to get great work done. But in case you're thinking, *Great? My organization isn't great!* just know that I've also seen these skills put to use in shitty organizations to get great work done; in small, private organizations to get great work done; in large, public organizations to get great work done, etc. You get the point.

Again, being a learning guy, I've structured everything in this book very much like I would structure a classroom experience. There are some stories and examples, some theory, and even some swear words to demonstrate how those theories come to life. After that, you will find some questions to think about and reflect on called Mirror Moments. And then, most importantly, *do*. I call these the Move to Action Moments—identifying the opportunities where you can actually apply what you're learning in this book or pay closer attention to your own behavior so you can move closer to the behavior that you and others want to see.

Whether you are thinking through the questions about what you have already done or debating what you would do in a hypothetical scenario, you will get the best results when you are willing to become a *scientist of your own behavior*. Take a moment or many moments to really think about how you behave, why you behave that way, and what results that behavior generates. And, as scientists do, stay objective, neutral, and curious throughout the process, open to whatever the results tell you and wherever they lead you. Using this mindset for self-reflection is one of the most powerful tools I have in my toolkit, and I think it will be for you too.

Finally, there is the "BUT WHAT ABOUT . . . !?" section, which will cover some of the most common troubleshooting scenarios. If you're giving things a good go and still struggling, that'll be a good place to start.

BUT WAIT, THERE'S MORE!

I know only about 10 percent of a person's learning and growth happens via formal methods (classes, reading books like this one, etc.) and the rest happens through coaching, personal support, and good old-fashioned trial and error. Given this reality, I've started a Facebook Group for people reading this book to ask questions, get feedback on their Mirror Moments or help with their Move to Action Moments, and—as they build skills or gather expertise to share—help others. If your "BUT WHAT ABOUT . . . !?" questions aren't covered in the book itself, I hope you'll join the group and ask them. And, since you'll be asking something *of* the group, I hope you'll also give something *to* the group by participating in the virtual classroom and discussion. The address is **www.facebook.com/groups/thisisnowyourgroup**. I'll remind you of this again at the end in case you forget.

The title of this book is a shout-out to a poster that Facebook's Analog Research Lab created and that deeply resonated with me. I loved it so much that I had it painted as a giant mural on the wall of Facebook HQ's orientation room. It reads, in giant blue letters, "THIS IS NOW YOUR COMPANY."

The content of this book is meant to take that concept down one level into the details. Your employer is *your* company. Your manager relationship is *your* relationship. The tough feedback you need to give or just received is *your* tough feedback. And if you act like your life is *your* life, I strongly believe that you will also generate results that benefit not only your own ambitions and goals but also everyone's. So, while this is indeed about your company, the emphasis is, appropriately, on *you*.

I wholeheartedly believe that everyone can be a leader and driver of their own best experiences, and I'm well aware that getting to that point is among the hardest work there is. And even if nobody else in your organization or your family or your church or your circle of friends can or will join you, you can still be that Culture Badass. And I'm here to help.

Let's get started.

3 | The Chapter about Being an Owner of Your Company

Maybe you're already on a rocket ship—awesome! Maybe you're on a team that feels more like a beat-up Chevy Malibu with two missing wheels and no AC on a hot August day but, despite all its obvious flaws, you see potential. Maybe you just started your first job out of college and you're still not totally sure how the whole "waking up at the same time every day" thing is going to pan out for you. Maybe you've been in the workforce since vinyl was cool (the first time) and you could write your own book about company culture and the individual's role in it. The fact of the matter is that you are sitting here, reading this book, and wondering how you can make your circumstances the best they can possibly be.

As a "Builder of Awesome People" at Facebook—a title I admittedly bestowed upon myself for the sole purpose of giving myself something huge to have to live up to every day—I had the humbling opportunity to tell the very newest employees to immediately begin thinking like owners of the company. This was often met with a healthy combination of enthusiasm and fear. Ownership is exhilarating and scary like that.

Technically speaking, of course, shareholders owned the company—maybe they own yours, too. And sure, the longest-tenured and most senior people usually had the largest *financial* ownership in Facebook, as they likely do in most companies. That's fine—I wasn't talking about actual financial ownership of the company. I was talking about ownership in the behavioral sense. Owning the full responsibility of the impact of your behavior on the culture of the organization at large.

It was a challenge to those newest employees to do things differently. In almost every company, organization, team, or relationship, it's normal and often accurate to think that our voices and our influence—particularly on the first day—aren't as valuable as those of the CEO or the people who have been around or involved the longest. I'm here to tell you—as I told thousands of them—to stop thinking like that. Acting like anything other than an owner in those early days means that you'll likely never act like one at any point down the road, either.

One of the main drivers of this reluctance to act like an owner, I think, is that we live in a culture that increasingly celebrates utterly false modesty.

"Oh, I'm just a such-and-such in the so-and-so division at Corporation, LLC. I'm a nobody, really."

EXCUSE ME, NO. NEAUX. ABSOLUTELY NOT.

This type of "modesty" seems, increasingly, to be expected in our culture. People who downplay their relevance (or exaggerate their irrelevance) are generally seen as humble, and people who shout about their impact from the rooftops are generally seen as assholes. And since most of us want to be seen as humble and not assholes—especially by new coworkers, bosses, or friends—we opt for this weird abstraction of humility.

But what this self-deprecation instills can have lifelong implications. It often solidifies the feelings of inadequacy that we can all face every day of our lives and, on our hardest days, are tempted to believe. It tells other people that you really don't think you have any sort of influence—that what you do all day every day doesn't really matter in the long run. And, to complete the vicious cycle, it makes us feel better about *not acting like owners.*

When you think the work you do doesn't matter, then eventually it won't matter. And neither will you.

And it's true—we live in a world where we're all essentially replaceable. What sets outstanding people apart is their ability not simply to *do* their jobs—whatever those jobs are—but also to represent themselves, their ideas, their values, their products, and their companies in ways that honor as many best interests as humanly possible. That representation goes far beyond simply crunching numbers or going to meetings or checking things off to-do lists. It means carrying yourself as a person of influence, a listener, and a communicator. It means becoming a role model of the values of the company you work for, the people you surround yourself with, and the ideals that you collectively aspire to. Like it or not, the success or failure of any organization or company—and their product—depends on the individual behavior of every employee. You.

Yes, you are that important.

Remember what I said earlier about speaking to visiting companies or conference attendees about organizational culture? I could almost always see them making the fatal error—shrugging off these simple realities because they didn't actually work at Facebook. "Facebook is different," they would say. "Facebook is a social media company. Of course it's important for Facebook employees to represent themselves on social media in a way that benefits Facebook." Sure, any employee at a social media company has a built-in platform that ties directly into the work they do. But in a lot of ways, so do you. If you live in the same city as your office, chances are you are interacting every single day with people who know your employer, know other people who work at your company, and know what your company does.

What set Facebook apart wasn't that we were guaranteed to be awesome. I'm confident that even Mark would admit that every big company has to suck at least a little. It's just the nature of large organizations, after all. That is life—there is no perfect company, there is no perfect team, and there is no perfect project. The goal of the CEO (and you) isn't to make it not suck at all, but to suck a bit less. To take unbearable things (loooong meetings, for example) and make them a bit more bearable. Throwing your hands in the air and declaring that your job or your team or your employer sucks is not an option, since doing so admits that you must suck, too.

What set Facebook apart was that we accepted that *our* culture was *everyone's* job, and that every contribution either made us better or worse. Every email, every meeting, every project, every door held (or not) combined to make up our culture.

I'll repeat that because I think it's easy to overcomplicate:

> ## Culture is the sum total of all the things that every person in the organization says or does in the process of getting things done.

With this understanding comes intense responsibility. Huge successes can be born from one person's understanding that, no matter their job title, they are an integral part of the success of their company. Similarly, one person can cause a major shitstorm—just ask the CIA whether or not Edward Snowden had an impact on their agency as a whole. But way beyond the sensational, each of us has an enormous impact on the people around us, at work, at home, on the subway, on the freeway.

Think, for example, of the most pessimistic person you've ever worked with. You know who I'm talking about. The type of Debbie or Donald Downer who drags the mood of a room down just by their mere presence. Did they whine to you about the latest team award? Did they suspect that forces were conspiring against them when they didn't get the last promotion? Did they complain that the food in the cafeteria got worse and worse every day? Now think of how many other people that person interacted with—suddenly, a whole network of employees has a framework for distrusting their coworkers, and maybe a couple of them spout it themselves, ad infinitum. We brush this type of person and those types of complaints aside, and we pretend that their opinions don't matter. But that is exactly how one person can change a culture for the worse. One snarky, unhelpful comment at a time.

This is not to say that your experience at any company will be smooth sailing. Any company that pretends to have it all figured out is feeding you a delicious platter of *le bullshit*. Maybe you won't get a promotion you really feel you deserved. Maybe you will see a project go off the rails after you repeatedly tried to save it. Maybe your boss will have that really annoying habit of never reading past the first sentence of your emails, maybe your teammates will drive you crazy with their gum-chewing, maybe the work you do will seem mundane after a while, or maybe your company will be involved in the type of dramatic scandal that only *Dateline NBC* can cover. The end result is the same: every action you take makes a company better or worse. Period.

This is the part where people are often tempted to silently say to themselves, *It's cool. I'll just fly below the radar. Stay agreeable, stay neutral. Stay out of trouble so I don't cause any problems and can go home to watch Netflix in peace.*

This is unacceptable.

Let me repeat for the people in the back: NEUTRALITY IS NOT ACCEPTABLE.

If somehow you manage to actually have a neutral impact on anything in life, you should most likely be fired for not contributing. Why? Neutrality involves silencing yourself when things go wrong. It involves not telling people things they desperately need to hear. It involves not being your true self because you fear people's opinions of you. Notice how those "neutral" actions become inherently negative? I can promise you those inherently negative actions, the passive-aggressive swallowing of your potential, will not only harm the company—it will also harm *you* in the long run. It will limit your career and your life and your happiness and your sanity.

It's that big of a deal.

This also doesn't mean you need to suddenly become Pollyanna. Owning the joint on day one doesn't mean being inauthentic and positive all the time, and it certainly doesn't mean you need to lie to people to protect their real or perceived delicate egos. Quite the opposite, in fact. You've been hired to contribute to your company, and if you see something going wrong *it is your job* to make it right. And sometimes that will involve long nights, a healthy dose of swearing, and more than a little stress. Avoiding those difficult times is impossible. But the fact of the matter remains: Your words and behaviors help shape the world around you. You are part owner of your workplace. Does a CEO have time to bitch about how someone messed up and if they'd just done as they were told in the first place the company wouldn't be in the mess it's in now? No. Not if they're a good one, anyway. When good CEOs find out there is a problem, they want to know what steps are being taken to fix it. And, I'd argue, they build organizations where the people who see the problem fix it first and then debrief their leaders after there's been a lesson or two learned about what happened and why.

They, like the rest of us, really don't have time or patience for anything that isn't moving the situation forward and making things better, but the major difference between us isn't found there. The difference is that taking action is their first instinct, not their fifth or tenth.

Here's the good news: Taking ownership of the company on the first day will have lasting benefits beyond your day-to-day work life. Acting in a way that embodies the values of the organization you work for is more than likely going to involve being compassionate, professional, and resourceful. Those are the types of skills that will strengthen all your relationships and make you a better person in general. Even if you're not the brains behind the next app or the negotiator sealing the deal on a major acquisition, your behaviors, attitudes, and priorities set the tone for your work and the work of your peers. Additionally, you're setting an example of how you want to be treated, both in and out of the workplace.

Again—the culture of a company and, indeed, the world is the sum total of *everyone's* behavior, and the simple fact of your existence empowers you to contribute to that.

But let's not use that word. Empowerment *sounds* lovely, but it still implies that you have a choice as to whether or not to use that power. I don't want you to feel *empowered* to think and act like an owner, or to use any of the other skills in this book.

I want you to feel *required* to do so.

Throughout this book, I will require you (see how much better that sounds?) to consider your own behaviors—your automatic reactions to day-to-day challenges. Are any of them negative or destructive? If so, what emotions or patterns do those behaviors validate? Maybe you don't know the answers to those questions just yet. Maybe you have been on autopilot up to this point in your life, and you need to ask a friend or coworker to help you figure out all the crazy shit you do. I'm guessing you might have a few friends who'd be more than willing to tell you all the ways you can be an ass. Thankfully, I do! The point is that you have the power to change things around you—including the culture of your organization, your family, your church, your social circle—but you will only achieve true change if you start with yourself, and that requires some pretty powerful self-reflection.

You haven't simply been hired to do a job. You've been tasked to be a part of a movement. People are counting on you to solve problems, to effectively make processes run more smoothly, to envision the future, to secure the present. To make it what you and your team will want in the future. They are counting on you to make your company better than it was when you found it.

So welcome. You are now an integral part of how things move forward. You own the direction this place goes from here on out. We work together as equal partners or not at all.

This is now your company, your life, your manager, your

hard conversation, your failure, your success.

Ready to act like it?

MIRROR MOMENTS

1. Think of a moment at work (or school, or in a group of friends) where you knew there was an opportunity for someone to step up and own a problem that you *didn't* seize. What was the nature of it? What prevented you from stepping up?

2. Think of a similar type of moment where you *did* seize that opportunity, no matter how small it might seem now. What were the circumstances? What *required* you to step up? What was different from the scenario in the previous question? (Hint: It's usually the other people involved, the scope of the perceived problem, the complexity of the solution . . . but it's also in many cases just plain old fear. See chapter 10.)

3. If I asked your peers or leaders if you were seen as a culture leader (someone others look up to and whose behavior sets examples for others to follow) or culture spectator (self-explanatory), which would they say best describes you? Why? Are you OK with that description?

MOVE TO ACTION MOMENTS

○ You notice a recurring meeting doesn't seem to add any

value to getting important things done. While everyone in the room *knows* it, nobody *says* anything.

○ There's a process that everyone in your team needs to follow in order to get work done smoothly, but there's no training for it and learning how to do it correctly is a stressful experience for new people. People laugh and say it's a form of initiation to the team.

○ There's a client who's pretty regularly rude to you and to your coworkers, but because this client brings business and revenue, everyone seems to think that the behavior is one of the costs of doing business.

Since this is the first chapter with these scenarios, here's how I'd like you to use both the Mirror and Move to Action Moments. First of all, if they're hard to answer or seem really tough to solve, good—this is by design. I didn't say that this work would be easy, just worthwhile. Don't answer the questions quickly just for the sake of answering them, either; it's fine to read a question or a scenario and then put some heavy thinking into your answers. It's complex, and I get that. It's worth taking some time to get to a real and useful answer instead of just getting an answer quickly.

On the Move to Action Moments—take a blank sheet of paper. At the top of the left-hand side of the page, write the word "Spectator," and on the top of the right-hand side of the page, write "Leader." Nobody is going to judge your answers here, but it's important not to just write what you'd do in an ideal world (as a leader). You also need to understand and name what spectators do, and what you, yourself, have done when in spectator mode. We all have the ability to be both. Categorizing the behavior isn't an exercise in judgment, necessarily; it's an opportunity to better understand the difference between being someone who gets things done and being someone who watches others get things done.

That way, when Move to Action Moments happen, you'll be better prepared to see the patterns of behavior that show up in leaders you want to emulate and, similarly, the patterns of behavior that show up in spectators that you will want to minimize or avoid altogether. With both sides identified, it'll be clearer where you need to move from spectator to leader and what that shift will look like.

And, of course, you can always pop into the Facebook Group if you want or need help, ideas, some tough love, or a virtual high five or hug.

4 | The Chapter about Organizational Stockholm Syndrome

One of my favorite things to ask a big group of new people in orientation—or attendees in a talk about organizational culture—is to list all of the things they hate about unhealthy organizations. Ideally, these are organizations they'd previously been a part of but left for one reason or another. Let me tell you, these lists can be loooong. When they are done, I ask them a very pointed question:

At what point do you think the founders of these terrible organizations decided that they wanted to create shitty workplaces that people would ultimately leave, taking their talent, ambition, and cultural and product knowledge with them?

There usually aren't any answers to that one.

In most cases, as soon as I ask that question, people realize what I realized long ago: companies aren't created to suck but can become sucky when people—that includes you and me—behave in sucky ways. So if nobody starts an organization intending it to suck, the suck must happen when people join it. When they let it happen. When they decide to ignore the problems they should fix.

In short: organizations start to suck because we start to suck.

And if you want to act like the owner we just talked about you acting like in chapter 2, this is where the work begins.

I know, I know, acknowledging that you sometimes suck is tough. It's far easier to point the finger at the person next to you, or your boss, or the CEO, or me! And hey, if it's any consolation, sucking is an affliction we all face at one point or another in our life or career. And joining a company and helping to make it suck is a practice as old as gatherings of people, an affliction I like to call Organizational Stockholm Syndrome.

* * *

First, some background.

In spring 2011, about a month after I started working at Facebook, I was asked to start leading the orientation for new employees—the n00b orientation, as we called it—that I had just barely completed myself. Both Facebook and the learning team I'd joined were small and scrappy, and the new hires weren't going to onboard themselves, so I said, "Why the hell not?" and jumped in.

This early honor/terrifying responsibility included the incredible opportunity to meet and, more importantly, work with several long-term employees who served as the culture-carrying guest speakers that packed our agenda. Since Facebook orientation was and is largely about the company's culture and mission more than benefits and rules, these speakers helped new employees get an incredibly valuable and honest sense of who we were and who we aspired to be as an organization, and how to contribute to that outcome from day one.

One of those leaders was a gentleman named Pedram Keyani, an early software engineer and culture leader extraordinaire. It was from him that I learned to ask the question that started this chapter and which I will now pose to you:

What are some things you have hated in your previous organizations?

Take a minute. I'll wait. When you have your list, write it down here—then turn the page.

If you're like me, you probably came up with some or all of the following cultural characteristics of unhealthy organizations. In my experience, the list below would be the "greatest hits" I've seen over the years I've spent in leading conversations about organizational behavior and dynamics:

- Passive-aggressiveness
- Resistance to innovation
- Too much bureaucracy
- Rewarding effort over impact
- Ass-kissing = career success
- Too many meetings that don't matter
- Not enough meetings about things that do matter
- Low or no leadership accountability
- Bad leadership in general
- Poor interpersonal communication
- Bad managers
- Overly competitive coworkers
- Unclear success criteria
- Too many assholes
- Not enough reward for impact
- Too much reward for negative impact

Class after class took the bait. They thought we were going to lead them in a rousing game of "Let's bitch about big companies that suck so we can juxtapose their shittiness against Facebook's awesomeness!" But after they came up with their list, we had them. The new employees had essentially made a list of cultural attributes they had either actively or passively contributed to in their previous jobs, even if they hated those things and couldn't wait to get away from them.

Yes, *contributed to*. If you and I hate the things on the list but don't actively contribute to a solution, our passivity is an endorsement. We are, I'd argue, the biggest part of the problem because, while most big problems are started by small numbers of people—let's call them assholes—they are perpetuated and grow because of the ambivalence and silent approval that come from the non-asshole majority.

"Hey," we would always say in closing. "If you didn't like any of that crap in your previous companies, don't bring it here."

It was a powerful reminder, and yet, as the company grew, those behaviors did start trickling in. It wasn't a question of if they would happen, but when—and, most importantly, what we would do about it when they did.

Let's be clear: it was easy to list the behaviors themselves during an inspiring orientation talk. I mean, come on, who doesn't like complaining about things that suck? I also realized that any well-intentioned, brand-new employee who would bring those behaviors to our company in the first place was more than likely doing so subconsciously. But figuring out why it happened wasn't as important as figuring out what to do about it, and it was a big part of my job to get them to understand that if they didn't acknowledge the fact that they had contributed to those behaviors in their old companies, they were very likely doomed to repeat them.

Not on my rocket ship!

This is where the Stockholm syndrome part comes in. In every company I've worked in or consulted with, I've found that people (myself included) are generally very quick to identify the behaviors or norms—acknowledged or otherwise—that they hate about a team, division, or organizational culture. They are just as quick to disavow any role in creating or sustaining them. And that's why we employ behaviors that recreate it.

Let me give you a personal example. When I started at Facebook, *my* answer to the question was the one I put at the top of the list: I hate passive-aggressiveness. I'm aggressive-aggressive. When I left SF for NYC, one of the main things that convinced me to do it was a nonwork moment I had while absent mindedly walking down Fourth Ave from Union Square. I was committing the cardinal sin of being facedown in my phone and not paying attention to where I was going, and I ended up getting hip-checked by a local as he rushed by me. As he passed, he turned around and said, "Hey asshole, pay attention!" Right then and there. He didn't go home and write a blog post detailing the affront of our encounter, he didn't post on Facebook about how awful pedestrians in NYC were at walking—he just called me out in the moment it happened. When I realized how much I loved this directness, I couldn't help but yell, "Thank you!"—to which he turned around and winked and smiled. Two months later I lived in New York City.

So yeah, I hate passive-aggressiveness. And yet, when I really took inventory of my past behavior in other roles and companies, I could see where, when passive-aggressiveness was the cultural norm for getting things done, I quietly played along. Even excelled at it! Sure, I bitched and complained about it, too, but when push came to shove, I would ultimately grit my teeth and join in if it was clear that was the way things were going to get done.

I went to the "five meetings before the meeting that mattered" instead of calling out how all the extra time being spent not solving problems was a waste. When the meeting that mattered finally *did* come along, I often sat silently when others did the same, telling myself it wasn't *my* job to speak up. "Leave that to some more senior/tenured/risk-tolerant people!" I'd tell myself as I watched the problems continue or grow. And they almost always grew, which would then require me to gripe my way through a handful of additional meetings to bitch about how much of a waste of time it had all been. See the formula?

STEP 1: Hate the problem

STEP 2: Contribute to the problem

STEP 3: Blame others for the problem while absolving self

STEP 4: Inadvertently teach others how to contribute to the problem

STEP 5: Ensure the perpetuation of the problem forevermore

I've shared that example with many people, including lots of senior leaders from other organizations, at conferences like the one I spoke about in the introduction, when they visited Facebook, or when I visited them. Without exception, they all smiled sheepishly and nodded with that pained *Yeah, wow, that's real* look on their faces. They knew it was real, and so do you. Perhaps too real. The pained part of the look was because they, too, knew what I had known about myself—that I'd played along because in the moment it felt easy to do so. When the time comes, it is *so hard* to reckon with our own contributions to shitty culture.

But if we don't own our roles in these types of ridiculous organizational behaviors, we become active contributors to the problems we say we despise. And to make matters worse, we almost always blame everyone else and take none of the responsibility ourselves. It just takes someone pointing out that we do it to ourselves for the façade of *Not my fault!* to crumble away.

You, dear reader, are now armed with the combined sense of dread and relief that almost always coexist whenever you realize that the problem you face is *you*. For the record, *you* are what this whole book is about, and we're going to spend a lot of time on *you*, so get some coffee or a martini and a comfy chair–we're going to be here for a while.

It's never fun to hear that you suck, but it should be empowering (there I go, using the word I made fun of just a chapter ago) to hear that you own not sucking, too. And *not* sucking is awesome.

And the key to not sucking is simple: own your role. If you didn't fix the thing you disliked in your last company, you were at least giving it your silent approval and probably helping to perpetuate it. Full stop.

If you *don't* own that role, I can guarantee you that you're at higher risk of repeating those behaviors you despised in your old organization, not because you loved the role you played but because, after time, it became familiar to you. It became your comfort zone. It became normal.

Psychologists proved long ago that our brains love nothing more than relying on the familiar, even if we know in our heart of hearts that those familiar things are hindering progress in some way. And in the very worst-case scenario, if nobody calls you on it, you'll end up recreating the very environment you swear up and down you don't want in the place you just joined. That brand-new, shiny beacon of hope that is your new organization will become a dull, dingy, familiar, and depressing old lamp. The one that you inherited from an aunt that has chips and doesn't go with anything. And it will be your fault.

This way of looking at your own role in creating your reality at work has benefits outside of your work life. Think back to my encounter with my fellow pedestrian on the sidewalk in NYC. Had I not owned the fact that I wasn't paying attention, I probably would have been pissed the rest of my walk to work instead of thinking, *Yeah, I totally did what he just accused me of*. Bonus number two is that my acknowledging it made *him* happy, too, and instead of shaking his head and hating slow walkers he probably went through the rest of his walk thinking that the world wasn't quite as shitty as my walking skills were. Win-win.

This subtle but massive, tectonic, life-altering shift in how you think about your behavior and the way it impacts your experience is a vital part of the closure process of leaving your last organization. It is a critical part of your obligation as a new employee of any new team or organization you've joined, whether they've asked you to go through this exercise or not. After all, great leaders don't need to be told to do the right thing, they just do it.

Organizational culture is a powerful thing, and owning your role isn't so much about apportioning blame as it is about helping you adopt a powerful new point of view about how your behavior contributes to your own reality and the realities of your coworkers. *How* you get things done has just as much positive impact to your professional reputation and your career as *what* you get done along the way.

Make that contract with your new gig and the people in it. Boldly proclaim that you're an active player, not a passive victim. That you and everyone else you work with are now a part of a new deal, one in which you admit that you're human. That you want something better for yourself, your team, and your company. And that you're going to call out sucky behavior when you see it. Especially if the perpetrator is you.

People ask me about the secret to Facebook's well-known work culture. This is the not-so-secret answer: the employees—hopefully all of them—hold themselves to a standard that requires them to do better than they have done before. They give themselves and each other tough feedback when someone or something falls short. They acknowledge that if there is a failure, it's everyone's fault and everyone's responsibility to fix.

They acknowledge that as soon as one of them thinks, "It's OK to be an asshole! Everyone else will absorb my bad behavior!" the slippery slide into mediocrity will begin.

And finally, they administer the only known cure for Organizational Stockholm Syndrome—they acknowledge the roles they've played in directly or indirectly contributing to whatever they've hated about other sucky organizations. Even and especially if they silently enabled it. And then they commit to not repeating it.

MIRROR MOMENTS

1. On the list of things you wrote that you didn't like about a company—current or former—what role did you play in perpetuating the behaviors behind them? Why?

2. When opportunities to confront those behaviors came up, what held you back from taking ownership and doing it?

3. Which of these bad behaviors might you be at the highest risk of repeating (or enabling) in your new or current organization?

MOVE TO ACTION MOMENTS

(*Remember: the left-hand side of the page is for "SPECTATOR" behaviors and attitudes; "LEADER" behaviors and attitudes go on the right!*)

- You're having a meeting with your boss and, when you see a shortcut to getting your way, you start to feel the urge to use a tried and true (and unhealthy) tactic from your last company.

- A new coworker from a very laid-back organization joins your team and immediately rebels against any sort of structure or process that you've had in place since well before they joined.

- Your team has a consistently unhealthy way of dealing with conflict (avoiding it in the moment, talking shit behind people's backs instead of addressing behaviors head-on, forming factions along the different points of view about a problem, etc.).

BUT WHAT ABOUT . . . !?

Great, but what about when I backslide into old habits?

One of the things many trainers and coaches have their students/clients do is find someone they can partner with as they're trying to stop doing shitty things that hold them back. This is no exception! One of the reasons I told the story about hating passive-aggressiveness to SO MANY PEOPLE is that it all but guaranteed that one or more of them would hold me accountable if I ever actually did something passive-aggressive—consciously or unconsciously.

Find *your* Stockholm Syndrome Behaviors and find a person you trust—even if you're brand new, you can build trust quickly with other new people, so start there if nobody else comes to mind—and give them the things that you are aware you probably contributed to. Have a laugh about how horrifying it is to have to own the suckage you contributed to previous organizations. Swear to do better and give that person drama-free-guaranteed permission to call you out on it if you do it again.

OK, fine, I own the place and everything depends on me . . . but . . . what if I'm not having much luck holding other people accountable to this standard?

Again, this is where self-awareness and disclosure can be so important. Nobody loves talking about all of the shitty things we individually and collectively do to sabotage our organizations, so you have to approach the subject with care.

"Look, I hate that I didn't hold myself to a higher standard when people were being passive-aggressive and I joined in, but there's nothing I can do about that last organization. I can only do something here. I've admitted mine—what are yours?"

There is a significant amount of power in this type of honesty—ironically, though, we carry with us a ton of fear that others will judge us for being imperfect. It's ironic because it's these types of admission of humanity that endear us to others. And a good leader will always put themselves into the problem and then help find a way out of it.

5 | The Chapter about Not Being a Dick about the Duck

A senior employee came in at the end of my own orientation class to talk to the six of us who had started just one day before. He delivered a fiery speech about how much he hated entitlement and how pissed he was that someone in our fledgling Seattle office had recently taken issue with something about the carrots in the office's micro-kitchen. He then asked all six of us (and it was suuuuper uncomfortable being asked this question in such a tiny group with this dude staring you down):

"Why the fuck did we hire you?"

Have you ever been in an orientation where a senior leader stared you down on your second day and spoke to you like that? Neither had I. I was at least a tiny bit terrified, but I was *in*.

He didn't intend for us to answer him, though. He intended for us to answer *ourselves*. Daily. Why were we there, newly oriented, ready to get started? Why us? Out of the hundreds or thousands of people who had applied for our jobs, why were we the ones selected? It wasn't the carrots. It wasn't the shuttles that took us to and from our apartments in San Francisco and around the Bay Area. It wasn't the sushi that was served to us daily (yes, we used to have sushi—which was the only real reason most engineers ever came to our office on Page Mill Road, about a quarter mile from the engineering office on California Avenue) or the free headphones that our IT stocked in filing cabinets. It wasn't any of that stuff. We were hired to work our asses off and to connect the world. Everything else was, at best, secondary.

Facebook had about 675 million active users, was (unbeknownst to us at the time) a year away from one of the most scrutinized IPOs in history, and had become a "big" company of almost 1,800 employees—more than half of whom were in those two buildings in the Stanford Research Park in Palo Alto. We all felt the sense of urgency that our promising and admittedly daunting future entailed. We were on an incredible trajectory and really only getting started.

Throughout this talk, I nodded my head so vigorously that my neck actually hurt afterward. I left orientation fully commited to being the best me I could be and taking nothing for granted.

You probably can imagine being in my shoes that day, because you, like me, have been the new person on day one, right? Don't we promise to be the best versions of ourselves? Aren't we so happy, in so many cases, with how refreshing the new place seems to be, how thrilled we are to be there? He described the exact opposite of who I saw myself being in life, and definitely the opposite of who I planned to be at Facebook. He was describing . . . well, a dick. Someone I wouldn't want to work with, who the people I was joining wouldn't want to work with. And, clearly, someone who could exist even in a place like Facebook. It was hard to fathom on that second day, but possible nonetheless.

I swore up and down right then and there that I would never be that person. Ungrateful, unimpressed by all that was being given to me, arrogant about my place of employment and their obligation to serve my every need. Instead I would be grateful, always, for everything. And in the many years that passed since that second day, I was almost 100 percent successful.

Almost. Up to the ninety-day mark, I was successful in being grateful and awestruck and humble and patient, doing all the things good employees do when faced with overwhelming generosity—until I wasn't. At the ninety-day mark, I was a dick for the first time, and I spent the next several years telling thousands of new employees this cautionary tale in hopes that it would prevent them from repeating my mistake.

On that fateful evening, three months in, I was exhausted from the blistering pace at which Facebook operated, the tiny team with which we had to get so many things done, and the newness of everything—especially because at the time, *everything* had to be built from scratch. I stood in line for dinner, barely able to stand up, squinting at the menu placed at the entrance to the serving line, and let out an audible, dramatic sigh.

They were serving duck. For the second time in a week. And I was not in the mood. How could they?

WHO EATS DUCK CONFIT TWICE IN ONE WEEK!?

My indignation quickly, thankfully, turned to shame. Had I already, just three months in, become the person in the cautionary tale?

Fortunately, I was only dramatic and annoyed in my thought bubble, as the Facebook Culinary Team—then and now among the most revered teams at Facebook—was not serving duck again to personally screw me over. They were not serving anything for my specific needs, ever, because they were serving all of us. So, in addition to being annoyed at this menu repetition, I was now also more annoyed with myself. Despite my second-day best intentions, it was true: just ninety days in, I had failed, I had been that person. Was this the end of the honeymoon—so soon? I skipped dinner altogether and instead stopped and got some far crappier and more expensive food at the grocery store on the way home.

It left a permanent mark on me.

When I told this story in orientation to Facebook employees on their second day, their responses were almost always to laugh and be awkwardly shocked. That was by design, because I wanted them to find my behavior as utterly ridiculous as I did and because, as I stated after, they, too, would have their duck moments. They just would. We all do, don't we? Even if we're surrounded by the very best people, the very best benefits, the very best work environment, the very best school or church or coffee shop or or or . . . at some point, even the amazing becomes normal. Because we're humans before we're employees, and that's how humans roll.

Over time, I also learned that I should remind them to forgive themselves when it happens but not to let the moment pass without doing, as I and thousands of their coworkers had, a quick inventory of how ridiculously fortunate we all were every day to be given what we were. None of us deserved any of this. We would never work hard enough to deserve everything that the world had given us by way of our employment at Facebook—because, ultimately, it wasn't Facebook giving it to us; it was the people we served and who used our products every day. Facebook was the delivery service, but the outside world was paying the bill.

That final piece is incredibly important. As we grew, as many companies do, from a small, tight-knit group where everyone generally knew and felt accountable to each other and to a large organization filled primarily with coworkers who were strangers, we had people on any given day who were failing the "duck test"—and sometimes failing very visibly. Some of our teams even seemed to expect entitlement as a norm and behaved accordingly, like the times the Culinary Team put out signs apologizing to employees and visitors when the bananas in the micro-kitchens around campus—you know, for the hunger you'd undoubtedly feel between meals—on any given day *weren't organic*.

I know. It wasn't real life.

Because my moment and many others' moments of entitlement seemed to revolve around food, I often thought of Chef Josef Desimone, one of the early culture leaders I looked up to at Facebook. Josef was a rock star in the culinary world. He had dozens of tattoos and an undying affection for pickle-backs (a shot of whiskey followed by a chaser of pickle juice, a drink I fell in love with), and while his physical appearance and presence made him interesting, his unapologetic and some-times very loud disdain for culture-abusers made me love him. We lost him in a tragic motorcycle accident in the summer of 2013, and I knew he'd have been mortified by and would have actively engaged with anyone he witnessed being ungrateful or acting entitled.

But Josef wasn't around to be the culture carrier; it was up to us. And, as one of my favorite posters at Facebook constantly reminded me—"Nothing at Facebook Is Somebody Else's Problem." So I worked hard to hold myself and others to a standard that would make him proud. When flashes of entitlement happened, I'd remind people about the duck. I didn't have to push too hard—it's probably one of the things I'm most known for by those thousands of employees to whom I gave that talk. I implored them to recall it, to honor the amaz-ing legacy that Josef had built at Facebook and the massive amount of work he and everyone else in the company had put in to provide for us and help us provide for each other. And to honor this, not just by not being a dick about the duck but also by living up to his legacy of cultural leadership, ownership, and humility about the ridiculous bubble world we all knew—on some level—we were fortunate to live and work in.

Remember—a company's culture is defined and rede-fined day in and day out by the behaviors and attitudes of its employees. Gratitude and entitlement are *both* infectious, and if you allow yourself to feel and behave in an entitled way, you also have to be willing to tolerate the same in everyone else you work with. Being humble about what you are given doesn't mean that you in no way earn it, either; after all, my coworkers and I worked really hard day in and day out to build Facebook. But lots of people who worked just as hard if not harder than we did didn't get treated nearly as well by their employers, so being humble about it was an important way to stay grounded.

I've shared this story externally to many more thousands of people, and while I completely understand that not every-one in the world can relate to being given so much, the impor-tance of gratitude is universal. There are lots of things in every company that you can be a dick about if you're not mindful, if you're not grateful for what you have. And while I am one of the people who is quick to give feedback to any-one whose work I think can have more impact, to share ideas about how to serve employees or customers or partners better, I never, ever forget to say thank you first, and not to be a dick about the duck.

And I do it for Joey.

MIRROR MOMENTS

1. What are the things in your organization—perks, benefits, maybe even other people—that you have allowed yourself to take for granted? How has that entitlement shaped your behavior or influenced the behavior of others around you?

2. Have you had any "duck moments"? How did you handle them? How might your handling of those moments contribute to how others view you, especially if you didn't handle them well?

MOVE TO ACTION MOMENTS

○ You're in the office copy room and, when you go to pick up a print job, you notice that (for the second time in a month, no less!) the paper in the printer has run out and nobody has bothered to refill it.

○ You see a senior coworker abusing—and then bragging about abusing—a perk that everyone values and nobody wants to lose.

○ You have an idea for a great perk that would cost the company some money but could also significantly improve productivity (and therefore morale).

BUT WHAT ABOUT . . . !?

I worry sometimes that I come across as being self-righteous when I try to model this non-dickish behavior, especially when I call people out on it. What is that all about?

Well, it might be about you being self-righteous. One of the best ways you can get other people to shape up their behavior is to acknowledge that you understand why they might want to do things the way they're doing them—indeed, that you may have acted the same way at one point—but that you don't think it's a good way to continue doing things. This is why it was important for me to share my duck moment as an opener to talking about entitlement. By showing that I wasn't perfect but also that I held myself to a better standard than my worst behavior could demonstrate, it was easier for people to hear that "lecture" from me.

My company is very small, and we are on the tightest budget imaginable (meaning no duck—no nothing!). How does this chapter relate to that sort of company?

I've worked at that company, too. Now that I'm self-employed, the perks have all gone away. But one of the most valuable perks that we all take for granted in some way is the people we do our work with every day. Our coworkers, our clients, the people who greet us in the lobbies of our buildings or who clean up our messes long after most of us have already called it a day. So even if you have not a single free organic banana to your name, you still have coworkers and others around you who are worth so much more. They're your duck, and you shouldn't take them for granted.

PART TWO
YOU AND OTHERS

6 | The Chapter about You, Your Manager, and a Fifty-Fifty Relationship

While much of this book is focused on you, your stuff, and your role in organizations, I couldn't actually write a book about building an awesome company without including a robust chapter on the massive role that management (that means your manager *and you*) plays in the process. There is, after all, a widely repeated saying out there that people don't leave companies, they leave managers. While I'm not sure that's 100 percent accurate, it *is* the reason that organizations of all types, sizes, and missions dedicate huge amounts of resources to training, coaching, and managing managers. And yet, despite these huge investments, most companies still don't get management quite right. People still leave those companies and those managers despite all their efforts.

So, because this is so important to you and to your company, it's worth spending some time talking about the role you can and really *must* play if you want your relationship with your manager to work for you and your career.

I'll start off by acknowledging the obvious: lots of managers, with or without your help, suck. But lest you think they suck because of something you said or did, let's be clear: managers who suck usually suck because they have no idea what they're doing, and they're terrified of admitting it because someone already gave them the big promotion. In many companies, the thinking behind promoting someone into a management role goes something like this:

Observation #1—Sue is a great engineer. Larry is a great salesperson!

Observation #2—Clearly Sue will be great at managing other engineers and Larry will be fantastic at managing salespeople. Let's promote them!

And then they do. Seriously, that's about it. Sure, maybe there are formal application processes to follow and perhaps employees will have to interview for the roles in order to get them, but for the most part, companies just assume that if someone is good at doing a job, they will therefore magically be equally amazing at managing, coaching, and directing other people doing that job.

With all we know about people management and how hard it is to do well, it's stunning that we regularly make such terrible decisions about whom to actually move or promote into those roles.

Yet here we are.

Now, this isn't to say that people who excel at sales or engineering can't also excel at managing salespeople and engineers—they can and often do. But it's nowhere near that simple. More on this in a bit.

Let's assume now that your manager is one of these people—promoted into a role for which they might be ill prepared and bumbling, or even well prepared theoretically but not yet well versed in all that is *you*. Now consider your relationship and your contribution to it (or lack thereof). Think about it—have you ever taken the initiative, proactively sat down with your manager, and said, "Hey, since you're managing me, we should probably talk about what that's going to look like, what I'm going to need from you, and what you're going to need from me in order to make this work for us both."

If you're being honest, the answer is probably a resounding no. But why? If the old adage about the manager-employee relationship being the most important of all is true, why don't we actually talk to our managers about what that's going to look like? Even organizations with mediocre or downright bad managers usually have some sort of expectations about what their managers should be doing, and yet most employees think it is the manager's job to approach this conversation. If he or she doesn't initiate it, the conversation doesn't happen.

Pardon my French, but THIS IS SO FUCKING FRUSTRATING! How many roles have you ever wanted to take with zero conversation about what success would look like? How many people, if you're a manager, have you ever told, "You know what, I'm not going to tell you what I expect of you, let's just see how things work out."

HOPEFULLY NONE.

And yet millions and millions of manager-employee and employee-manager relationships suck because people play a game of conversational chicken with regards to expectations.

We expect that it's our manager's job to initiate this incredibly important and relationship-defining conversation; if they don't, we assume they don't want to talk about it, and so we don't. And our managers are often terrified of fucking up and figure that they're just going to do what they think would work for *them* and . . . hope for the best? It's perplexing.

It's also why so many of these relationships are terrible and why so many expectations go at best quietly unmet and at worst horribly and *loudly* unmet. The icing on this crapcake is that both parties end up blaming the other and then repeating the pattern in a new role or relationship (see the previous chapter about Organizational Stockholm Syndrome, as it applies here in spades).

But not you, not anymore. You are half of the relationship, and you can't look yourself in the mirror and say your relationship isn't largely dependent upon your willingness to assert yourself and your needs and to encourage your manager to do the same.

Building a great employee-manager partnership is possible and necessary. One of the things that informed a lot of the subsequent work I did on manager development at Facebook was work that the incredibly talented People@ team (what Facebook calls HR) did to help the company articulate what it wanted and needed managers to do. To build this list, they actually partnered with employees—managers and individual contributors alike—and asked them how they thought managers at Facebook should be measured. They came up with seven management behaviors that they felt would represent managers and their employees at their best. I was elated when the head of the People@ team, Lori Goler, decided to share the list publicly in 2016, as I think it can help you, too. The steps are:

1. Show care for what is most important to each person's experience

2. Support people in finding opportunities to grow and develop based on areas of strength and interest

3. Set clear expectations for individuals and teams

4. Give clear, actionable feedback on a timely basis

5. Provide the resources people need to do their jobs well and actively remove roadblocks to success

6. Hold people and teams accountable for success

7. Recognize people and teams for outstanding impact

If you looked at that list and said, "Well, none of that is rocket science," you'd be right. It's not, nor should it be. It's not unlike many other lists of managerial expectations I've seen from other companies. But there are a few things that are worth pointing out here in terms of how the list has really come to life in meaningful ways.

First, when we started communicating these expectations in classes, we didn't "teach" them in the traditional sense. Since these expectations take the form of outcomes rather than checklists, we were very deliberately letting *managers* decide how to meet them. After all, how you show care for an engineer's experience differs, in many ways, from how you do the same thing for someone working in finance. Neither is better or worse than the other, just different. And we wanted our managers to have the flexibility to adapt what they did not only to their unique teams but to the individuals on them. Because management at Facebook is a partnership, we taught these expectations to everyone in the company, giving everyone an equal sense of urgency for owning their contributions to meeting or exceeding them.

> Whether becoming a manager in your company is a promotion or a lateral move, managing your half of the relationship is **critical** if you're going to play a leading role in your own career.

What follows is some of what I've learned over the years teaching this and similar content to thousands of people in multiple organizations around the world, expectation by expectation. Sure, I'm using Facebook's list here, but as we covered already, expectations of managers at most companies fall along similar lines. What is different here is that I believe wholeheartedly that you can accomplish a lot more—regardless of your role—if you take an ownership role in this relationship. It's by no means an exhaustive list of everything you and your manager need from each other—that's *your* work—but it should hopefully give you some things to think about and ideas to implement, as you know yourself and your own managers/organizations better than I do. I hope it will get you started on thinking about what you need your manager to do for and with you, as well as what *you* should be expected to do to manage your half of the relationship.

After each expectation, there's space for you to make some notes about what you can do to build this relationship, one conversation at a time. Trust me, reflecting on this and coming up with a list of action items is easier than you think.

Show care for what is most important to each person's experience.

You:

- Your manager is not a mind reader. If you want them to care about what you care about outside of work, you have to be willing to share it. This is not only accomplished by something like becoming Facebook friends (though I'll admit my bias here—I wholeheartedly believe that the fact that it's normal to be Facebook friends with coworkers is one of Facebook's biggest not-secret-but-not-common weapons) but by being willing to talk about your life outside of work *inside* of work.

○ Own it when there are periods of time where your personal priorities take precedent—either by choice or by necessity—over your work priorities, and be realistic about how your performance changes as a result. Taking a long view of your experience at your company will probably mean that there will be times when you are really killing it and firing on all cylinders, and other times when you aren't because you have other things going on. Healthy manager-employee relationships can help make these periods feel less tumultuous, but they require honesty and self-awareness about trade-offs.

Managers:

○ Get to know people for who they really are. It's hard to show that you care about people if the only things you know about them are about their life and activities *at work*.

○ When you have one-on-ones, don't just ask how work is going, ask how people are feeling. Yes, *feeling*. If they're tired or frustrated or excited. You're a better manager if you know about it and can help manage the bad stuff out. Not knowing how someone is feeling doesn't make those feelings irrelevant—in many cases, it makes them *more* relevant.

○ Know that what's most important changes pretty regularly and that you have to continue to pay attention to and ask about it. This is especially true if your employees' lives outside of work are changing. For example—hundreds of Facebook's employees started having lots of kids in 2011 and beyond, and what mattered to their experiences at work shifted dramatically as a result. Fight your instinct to not want to talk about it and have those conversations.

What would you add and what should you clarify with your manager?

Support people in finding opportunities to grow and develop based on areas of strength and interest

You:

- Take responsibility for identifying your strengths. It's not your manager's or anyone else's job to do this for you, and they couldn't even if they wanted to because they don't know you as well as *you* know you. If you haven't already read the groundbreaking *First, Break All the Rules*, you might not know that playing to strengths is far and away the biggest driver of impact, sustainable high performance, professional fulfillment, and so on and so on. Read it. And then read *Now, Discover Your Strengths*.

- Pay attention to and be willing to talk about moving away from the work that weakens you—especially things that you are good or even *really* good at doing but don't enjoy. You may be able to achieve great results in the short term, but it won't be sustainable—you'll eventually burn out, and it'll be mostly your fault.

- ○ See chapter 9 for more.

Managers:

- ○ Understand your employees' strengths and manage to them relentlessly. See comment above about *First, Break All the Rules*—same advice applies. While you're probably already adept at judging performance (output), it's far more valuable to understand the underlying strengths that drive that performance (input) if you want to help people contribute their best work for the longest period of time.

- ○ Redirect people from work that weakens them. Because we are all capable of doing work that we don't enjoy if the rewards (visibility, pay, etc.) are good enough, we often neglect our lack of fulfillment in doing that work. When you see signs that people are doing work that weakens them, intervene where possible.

- ○ Remind them that their careers are their responsibilities. Don't allow yourself to care more about their development and growth than they do—it's not sustainable.

What would you add and what should you clarify with your manager?

Set clear expectations for individuals and the team.

You:

- ○ Contribute to the conversation about your and your team's goals—especially if you believe that your manager doesn't have important information about feasibility or resources needed or competing priorities or redundancies with the work of other teams. You are likely closer to the work that is being measured than your manager is—and that is by design—so use that expertise to help them craft expectations that are challenging, are meaningful, and, most importantly, enable you to do your best and most impactful work.

○ Communicate upward and don't wait for clarity to arrive from on high with a bow on top. If you aren't getting enough specific direction about what's expected of you or why, ask. *Ask, ask, ask.* At the end of a performance review period, you are going to suffer more than your manager likely will (as you're probably not the only person on the team) if you allow a lack of clarity about expectations to result in a lack of performance, impact, and, ultimately, reward.

Managers:

○ Acknowledge that *all goals are made up.* I used to tell managers in training at Facebook that Mark and Sheryl didn't have a golden book of expectations from which they tore out and distributed pages to our many teams. For me, this discovery was both liberating and terrifying. The most important thing to do is to take a stab at it. If you've set the bar way too high, bring things back into the stratosphere before people burn out. If you've set the bar too low, acknowledge that and dial up the intensity. I've not actually seen many goals survive an entire six- or twelve-month performance period, so if you and your team commit to reevaluating and adjusting as you go, this process will be much less painful and more accurate.

○ Involve the people doing the work in setting the goals. This is especially true the more senior your people are, as they'll inevitably get to the point where they know and can articulate what success is and should be better than you can for them. Engage them in setting the goals that they'll eventually be expected to meet.

What would you add and what should you clarify with your manager?

Give clear, actionable feedback on a timely basis

You:

○ If you're not getting enough feedback to do your job well and grow, ask for it. When I've taught classes on feedback at every company I've worked with, many employees blame their managers for a feedback deficiency, but when pressed admit that they don't ask for feedback when they're not happy with the amount they're getting.

○ Know that how you respond to feedback—both from your managers and others—has the biggest impact on the amount you'll get going forward and how honest and useful it will be. If you devolve into a hot mess at the slightest insinuation that you're human and have areas to improve, you're all but guaranteeing that people will shy away from being honest about your performance—to your face, anyway. Conversely, if you show a hunger for information about how you can grow, develop, and improve, people will give it to you.

○ If you struggle to react well to feedback, read *Crucial Conversations* immediately, if not sooner. More than any other resource, class, or book I've encountered in my career, it has helped people manage the emotional responses that derail results. And emotions are rarely higher than when we're receiving feedback.

Managers:

○ Above all else, you have to want the other person to be successful before you give them any type of feedback. This is true even when doing something as serious as putting them on a performance improvement plan or even terminating them. When people don't question your intent, they trust you more, and when they trust you, you can talk about anything.

○ Know that for most of us, even hearing the word "feedback" jump-starts the famous amygdala hijack (a.k.a. fight-or-flight mode) that the folks at VitalSmarts teach so beautifully in *Crucial Conversations*. So instead of saying, "I have some feedback for you," and all but guaranteeing that the person on the receiving end will have an instant *Oh shit!* reaction, say "Hey, let's talk about how _____ went . . ." Subtle difference in approach, but massive difference in outcome.

○ Give lots of both types of feedback—positive and constructive. When people complain that managers are bad at feedback, it's not usually one type, it's both. Feedback about great behavior begets more great behavior; don't rely on people knowing that they're doing great work or assume that they'll pick up on subtle cues. Be clear, always.

○ Know that when people respond negatively to your feedback—especially on a regular basis—it's likely because they don't trust you, not because you're wrong. Read or attend *Crucial Conversations* ASAP if you haven't already.

What would you add and what should you clarify with your manager?

Provide the resources people need to do their jobs well and actively remove roadblocks to success

You:

○ The three points below for managers apply equally to you. If your manager is giving you too much or too little direction, don't hope that their crystal ball will point it out to them on your behalf. Sit down and give them that feedback so they can realign their approach to give the results you need.

- If you are the roadblock—own it. Talk about it. Assume that others want to help you be successful and will be better equipped to do so if they know what (or who) is getting in your way.

- If you see resources being wasted or poorly allocated—be the person who points it out and works to solve it. Part of being closest to the work means you will often have the most information about what resources are needed or not needed. If you share that information freely, people will trust you with more resources and more control over how they're utilized in getting things done.

Managers:
- This will be some tough love—often, the biggest roadblock to your employees' success is *you*. Whether micromanaging (giving direction or being involved to a degree that is not needed) or undermanaging (being absent when you are needed), managers have the unique ability to really screw up how people get things done. Think of yourself as a resource that your employees can leverage when they need you, and get out of their way when they don't.

- The second biggest roadblock to success is frequently the employees themselves. Whether it's self-doubt or a conversation (or several) they're avoiding or not having successfully, there is a direct link between this expectation and the expectation about giving timely feedback.

○ Be honest about constraints and involve your employees in decisions about how to deploy scarce resources. No team I've ever worked with had an unlimited budget, staff, or timeline to get things done. Be honest about your limits so you can jointly identify how to accomplish things.

What would you add and what should you clarify with your manager?

Hold people and teams accountable for success

You:

○ Hold yourself to a very high standard and frame your accomplishments in terms of impact, not effort. The worst thing you can do for your own performance and growth is to define success in terms of how hard you try.

○ If you have interviewing responsibilities for *any* open position, hire people you think will be smarter/better/faster than you are so that you can learn from them and do your best work. If you hire people you think are worse than you so that you can look better by comparison, you're begging for your team and your company to suck.

○ Move on to new projects, new teams, even new roles when you're no longer interested in doing the best work at the level needed to be great. This isn't a bad thing—it's worse to stay in a job that you're no longer committed to than it is to leave it.

Managers:

- Holding the team accountable for success means rewarding impact, not effort. As soon as you create an environment where trying to accomplish something is on equal or greater footing than actually accomplishing something, you've boarded a one-way trip to mediocrity. When people succeed, recognize them for it and reward them accordingly, but when they don't, hold them accountable.

- Steve Jobs famously said that A players hire other A players, B players hire C players, C players hire D players, and so on. This is why holding people accountable is so important. Expect success and manage people (with feedback, coaching, direction) toward it as long as they're capable of and committed to succeeding.

- Manage employees out when they're not capable of or interested in success.

What would you add and what should you clarify with your manager?

Recognize people and teams for outstanding impact

You:

- Be clear about what types of recognition matter most to you and share that information with your manager, but don't expect a trophy for everything you do. The best way to get more recognition isn't by lobbying for it but by doing great work.

- Be conscious of how you achieve results. Bring other people along with you, and celebrate and acknowledge others who help you achieve goals. If you need other people to accomplish great things, it makes you bigger to call out their contributions, not smaller.

- Do not, under any circumstances, tell yourself that it's OK to be a Brilliant Asshole (see below).

Managers

- When people succeed at doing impactful work, be specific in your praise of not only what they accomplished but how they accomplished it. The best way to see repeated excellence is to be specific about what contributed to it. Encourage them to reflect on the same.

- Don't reward people who get great results at incredibly high costs. This is also what I call the "Brilliant Asshole Problem"; if you have someone who delivers great impact but pisses everyone around them off in the process, hold them accountable for the impact that their behavior had on results. If they can't deliver great impact without these opportunity costs, manage them out.

- Remember that our most consistent form of recognition is directly deposited on payday. Special or significant recognition should be saved for really big stuff—over-recognizing smaller things is actually a detriment to your team, not a benefit.

What would you add and what should you clarify with your manager?

* * *

At the end of the day, great managers cannot exist without great employees and great relationships, and the best way to have a great partnership-orientated relationship is to talk about what will make it succeed. It never ceases to amaze me that despite the manager-employee relationship being among the most important in any organization, we routinely tolerate the reality that the vast majority of those relationships form, perform, and dissolve with very little conversation about what makes them work and what each person contributes in order for them to do so.

Whether you have expectations like the ones I shared above or not, you can talk to each other about this critical relationship. Here's how I'd recommend you approach it:

○ If you haven't previously talked about this relationship, acknowledge that reality—even if you've been working together for ages. "I know this might seem like a weird activity, since we've been working together for a while, but I think our relationship will be the best it can be if we talk about what we expect of each other and how we will divide and conquer to make this work."

○ As you talk about expectations, give yourself feedback.

"One of the things that is very important to me is getting regular feedback, and I am realizing that I haven't asked for it as much as I should have, and have sometimes gotten upset instead of getting proactive." Be specific about things that really matter, even if it's a bit uncomfortable to do it. And ask how you can help produce outcomes, not processes. "I've been here a long time, but clarity about goals is still really important to me, and I can probably play a role in defining those goals. How can I help?"

- If you're the manager and your employee isn't meeting you in the middle, express that. "Sometimes it's hard to give you feedback because I think you assume I'm trying to be punitive instead of helpful. Can we work on some agreements about how we share feedback so that it's less daunting for me to give and for you to receive?"

- Recognize that this is an iterative process, like any relationship, and that your work here will never be "done." But great employee-manager relationships produce the greatest results, and while it may or may not always be true that people leave managers more than they leave companies, the secret to and responsibility for a great relationship lie in both of you.

MIRROR MOMENTS

1. If you haven't yet had a conversation with your manager about how you can best work together, what's holding you back?

2. How has your behavior made it harder for your manager to work with you (this includes things like *not* talking about what you need, *not* telling them when they're doing something wrong, etc.)?

3. Building on number 2, if there are expectations that you haven't met, what can you own about your role in that missed expectation to show that you feel a strong sense of accountability for and ownership of the relationship?

MOVE TO ACTION MOMENTS

- You've just joined a new organization and will be reporting to a manager who is very clearly busy and has eleven other employees reporting to her.

- Your manager regularly barfs feedback all over everyone, especially when he's stressed out. It's unorganized, reactionary, and—most importantly—unhelpful. He's done it to you twice just this week.

- Your goals for the next quarter are, quite simply, impossible, and your manager doesn't seem to grasp that fact.

BUT WHAT ABOUT . . . !?

My manager and I have a pretty strained relationship. We've never really gotten along well. Talking about this now will seem totally out of the blue and, frankly, a bit weird.

You're right! It's *super* weird that you've never had this conversation—probably, I'm guessing, a big part of the reason that you don't get along. And yeah, if you've been in an expectation-free relationship for quite some time, it's a given that those unspoken needs are going to go unmet a good portion of the time. And your silence on the topic is a huge contributing factor.

That doesn't mean you shouldn't have the conversation—it makes it doubly important that you do. What it *does* mean, though, is that you're going to have to acknowledge your role. Something like, "I've been reading this book"—you're welcome!—"and one of the things I've come to realize is that we've never actually had a conversation about how to work together. There have definitely been times that that lack of clarity has made it hard for me to work for you, and I'm sure made it hard for you to manage me. Can we set up some time to talk about this in more detail? I've put some thought into how I can do better here, and I'd love to get your insights on this too."

You've got it from here.

It's great that Facebook didn't make managing a promotion for its managers, but it is a big move at my company. How can I possibly make my manager care about what I need from them?

Ha! You can't. You can't "make" anyone do anything, really. But you can *motivate* them to care about it, and we all know that we're far more likely to go along with things that we see value in than we are with things that others just told us to do.

Again, look at the answer to the question above: there's a pretty solid "WIIFM" (What's in It for Me?) in there, sure, but also a huge one for your manager. If I'm the first one to tell you, forgive me, but you are probably *not* always easy to manage. If part of your pitch for having this conversation is that you want to make things better for *both* of you, the *power* differential between you and your manager will probably matter less than the *impact* differential that likely exists from you two not being on the same page.

The key here—and in most of these chapters—is curiosity. Approaching the situation with an appreciation for the unknown (namely, how your manager feels about your relationship) combined with a commitment to better outcomes (namely, improved functioning between you two) is a recipe for success in the vast majority of cases.

And to add icing to the cake: you'll help them be a better manager for everyone else reporting to them, too.

7 | The Chapter about the Gift Nobody Puts on Their Wish List: Feedback

I want you to imagine that we're passing each other in the hall. As I'm walking by, I say, "Hey, do you have a few minutes later today? I have some feedback for you."

Would you have the *OH SHIT!* moment that so many of us do when you hear that dreaded word?

I'm guessing yes. The good news is, you're not alone. The bad news is that in my entire career, at every company I've worked at, the vast majority of people I've encountered— sometimes including me—absolutely suck at giving and receiving helpful feedback. What is especially frustrating about this is that teaching people how to give and receive feedback is at the core of almost every professional and manager training curriculum I've ever seen—my own designs and others'—and the subject of hundreds of books. How are we still so bad at it in so many ways?

And if the thought of anyone stopping you in the middle of that hallway with the dreaded question above causes an *OH SHIT* reaction, you are almost surely, at least sometimes, in that "people who suck at receiving feedback" category.

As I mentioned earlier, this is something that I'm not impervious to either, even though I've been teaching classes about communication and feedback for years. One of those moments happened when I'd been at Facebook only a few months. I had been in a meeting where I passionately and vocally disagreed with the opinion of a very senior leader who, conveniently, wasn't in the room. I wasn't *only* sharing it because the person wasn't in the room—but if I'm being honest, I was probably a bit more forthcoming with my ideas because I felt like I could share them freely and others present seemed to agree with me.

But later that day or the next, my boss walked by me while taking a phone call. He paused, put his phone to the side, and whispered, "Hey, [leader name] wants to speak with you about that meeting." And, of course, the opinion I'd shared so passionately with the people present.

He then returned to his phone call, leaving me, well, having several *OH SHIT!* moments in his wake.

Now, you'd think, since I *teach this for a living*, I'd do that thing I'm constantly asking other people to do: go into scientist mode and think, "Hmm. I wonder what that feedback could be?"

Instead, I pretty much instantly pants-crapped. I immediately went to the dark place.

"I am so going to get fired."

"I shouldn't have been so bold so fast!"

"I'm too new to have opinions like this!"

"God, the move back to Chicago is going to cost a fortune!"

When I go full drama, I go all the way in.

This was, unsurprisingly, debilitating. I could think of little else in the coming days, which is about how long it took for me to actually connect with the senior leader in question to hear what she had to say. I did what most people (mistakenly) do in the period of time that elapses between learning feedback is out there and actually hearing the feedback.

1. I replayed the meeting scene in my head over and over, analyzing (and dramatizing, no doubt) every word I'd said and every word everyone else had said.

2. I built alliances in my head—who would be on my side and back me up? Who might possibly sacrifice me should the need arise?

3. I tried to figure out how to restate (a.k.a. water down) my points and walk them back so as to not appear too contradictory or contrarian.

It was exhausting.

To make matters worse, when we finally connected, she simply had a couple of clarifying questions about my point of view and wanted to get some additional feedback from me. Then she thanked me for sharing it all.

That was it.

THAT WAS IT!

I'd just wasted a ton of time and emotional energy creating a situation, problem, and reality that didn't exist.

Anyone with me? That's what I thought. This is why I tell myself and others all the time that when you have feedback for someone, give it to them ASAP. Don't do the feedback drive-by that I talked about above, because it can lead to a really crazy spiral for the receiver.

FOCUS ON THE FACTS

Before I go any further, I have to give credit to the incredible work done by VitalSmarts in their book and class *Crucial Conversations* (the two of which have been staples of both my career and thousands of my coworkers' across several employers). Their work and partnership have been invaluable in helping me understand and implement the tools necessary for creating culture that is better than it was, if not great, at accepting feedback.

Here's what we know for sure: for whatever reason, the word "feedback" elicits a physiological change in most of us. That *OH SHIT!* reaction is a type of fight-or-flight response, no matter how innocuous the feedback might be. And it's important to acknowledge that that response is almost never because of the person giving the feedback. In the example I shared about my boss and the senior leader, neither of them was responsible for my emotional reaction—that was allll me.

We also know that when we are in a heightened emotional state, we tend to deliver the worst results. This is evidenced by the number of hours and days I wasted worrying about the feedback I was going to receive and by all the more important things I either didn't get to or didn't do well because my entire existence was hanging in the balance until the feedback conversation happened. And it's as true for positive emotions as it is for negative emotions—ask anyone who's bought a timeshare because they loved their vacation soooo much, only to end up paying for their joy-driven decision with years of . . . payments.

As much as I don't blame anyone for my own emotional reactions to feedback or other types of criticism, my boss, knowing that these heightened emotional states are exacerbated when there aren't many facts to work with, could have added a few more details, helping me to help myself keep my emotions in check. Something like "Hey—[Leader] wants to follow up with you about the meeting the other day to get some more context about the ideas you shared." With these additional details—clean, pure facts and a lot less ambiguity—I can replace a fear-driven response with an open-minded curiosity about what the conversation might bring about.

Easy, right?

Of course not. But easier. And largely because of the omission of the dreaded word itself: feedback.

This came up again a few weeks later. Another senior leader in our sales organization asked me to come up with training on giving and receiving feedback more effectively. "But . . ." he asked reluctantly, " . . . could you call it something other than 'feedback'? Just come up with another word, something different?"

I was floored. The thought of taking the word "feedback" out of feedback training seemed counterproductive to me. In my idealistic state, away from the threat of actually being on the receiving end of any feedback myself, I had forgotten how powerful the word was—how derailing and distracting it could be when used in advance of even the simplest of conversations. I wondered: How was I supposed to help people do the hard work of accepting feedback without expecting them to understand and acknowledge their own emotional responses to the word itself?

We talked for a long time and landed on this: talking about feedback is hard, and changing the word wouldn't make it any easier.

It was one of the many times in my career I'd been wrong—changing the approach and eliminating the word *does* help. Let's look at another example:

You are in sales, and you and your boss went to a client meeting where you were pitching a new product to a group. The meeting was OK, but there were no firm commitments at the end, so it didn't really feel successful. You and your boss both know that you need to debrief that meeting, but it could go any of a dozen ways from that point. Which of the following three would you prefer?

1. As you're leaving the client site, your boss says "Hey, I have some feedback for you on that meeting." (UGH! Right?)

2. As you're leaving the client site, your boss says, "That meeting was just OK for me. Want to debrief how it could have gone better so we have a clearer path to success in the next meeting?"

3. Neither of you says anything. You pretend nothing happened until it comes up again randomly in a future one-on-one (or, worst-case scenario, as a line item in your next performance review).

It's important to note that all three of the above options happen all the time. And the first option might be totally fine if you and your boss are cool like that and the likelihood of emotions getting crazy is low. When most people complain about their manager or the feedback they receive, though, it's because the third option is so prevalent. It's hard to give and to receive good feedback when both parties are afraid to address the thing, defaulting to avoidance until a system (like a formal performance review) requires them to face things.

And yes, for the vast majority of cases, the second option would be the best: (a) It doesn't include the dreaded word—*feedback*, if we're not clear on that yet—so it doesn't immediately raise the emotional intensity; (b) it's honest right from the start but also immediately shifts to "better" and "success" as the focal points of the conversation; and (c) it shows the boss is about progress and improvement, not finger-pointing and blame.

If you're having that idealist objection ("But these delicate flowers need to be able to handle someone saying the word 'feedback' to them without crumbling into a pile of feels!"), I can only highly encourage you to abandon that thinking. I did, and I'm a better giver and receiver of feedback because of it.

Before we move on, though, I want to share another story about the incredible damage that can come from choosing option three (avoidance until forced).

It happened in one of the first *Crucial Conversations* training classes I taught at Microsoft. The class generally attracts such a bunch of wildcards—you never know why people are there. Many at Microsoft took the training because it was culturally prevalent to be somewhat passive-aggressive with hard conversations and employees wanted to learn how to speak more confidently. On the opposite end of the spectrum, when I started teaching it at Facebook, it was because people spoke up regularly and often too forcefully, so learning how to be direct but a little less blunt was more common.

At any rate, in both environments, this program inspired *lots* of interesting examples of conversations that had either gone terribly wrong or had been completely avoided. In this particular session, a woman walked in, sat right in the front row, and eagerly started flipping through her materials. I just knew she was going to be a participator. You know the kind. The Olympic gold medalist of participators. The *I'm happy to make sure this training solves all my problems* vibe clung to her. She did not disappoint.

In our two-day training, we got to know her situation with her mother-in-law *really* well. To sum it up briefly, the mother-in-law had said something snarky on her wedding day—you know, a day when emotions are totally running low and nothing ever goes wrong or causes stress, right? Joking aside, this thing was something that had clearly, deeply impacted her. All her work in training revolved around how this encounter was affecting her relationship with her mother-in-law, how difficult it was for her to move on from it, and how fearful she was about finally speaking her mind. Nevertheless, she made some good progress and got *lots* of moral support from me and her fellow participants. When she left the class, she was firm in her resolve to have The Conversation.

One of the downsides of my type of work is that I rarely get to see or hear what happens next, and I definitely had a few moments in the coming years where I wondered how that conversation had gone, if it had happened at all. Almost five years later, I got my answer when I ran into her in the hallway at work. She was visibly excited to see me. She told me she'd confronted her mother-in-law about what she'd said on her wedding day, and they had worked through the issue thanks to my class. She even mentioned that the mother-in-law's relationship with her grandkids had improved as a result—and because everything had gotten so much better, she would be attending one of the kids' upcoming graduations.

I wondered—graduation from *what*? How long had this been going on?

"Oh," I said. "How old are your kids?"

"They're in college," she answered.

It was one of those eyes-popping-out-of-your-head moments. She had waited until her children were in college before having this conversation? I felt myself doing the math in my head. This interaction had happened on her wedding day. How many days, holidays, conversations, vacations, *moments* had been ruined because of this unresolved conflict? The emotional cost of this was overwhelming.

And yeah, I admit, I got super judgy for a minute. But before you and I quickly bemoan her terrible procrastination and dismiss hers as a one-off story, keep in mind that many of us—maybe even you—have a "mother-in-law situation" of our own. The truth is, we often tell ourselves that the cost of having an important, difficult conversation is too high. So we don't do it. And that choice affects us in all kinds of personal and professional ways. In many cases, the lingering side effects of that avoidance can become incredibly high.

Let her story be a cautionary tale for all of us. It's unbelievable to me how long we will bear the burden of unshared feedback and what prices we will pay in order to avoid dealing with it. I've almost never seen someone not feel an incredible sense of relief when that feedback is finally out in the open. Stunted relationships, slow or no progress, perpetually hurt feelings, massive misunderstandings—these things and many more are the side effects of choosing option three, so trust me: don't do it. Get the help or the training you need to push through that fear. Even if sharing the feedback or having the tough conversation doesn't solve the problem—indeed, some problems really do go unsolved—you will sleep a million times better if you're no longer carrying it alone.

CRUCIAL QUESTIONS ABOUT CRUCIAL CONVERSATIONS

One of the other counterintuitive things I've learned about feedback over the years is that it is often much harder to give feedback than to receive it. Let that sink in for a second.

It is harder for many of us to give feedback than to receive it.

The reasons, scientifically speaking, are somewhat obvious. Telling someone something they might need to hear but don't *want* to hear takes courage on your part. Speaking up in a meeting to highlight a disagreement or different point of view, particularly with someone who might be more senior than you, takes guts. The receiver of the feedback simply has to listen, thank the person for the feedback, and move on with their day.

Of course, this isn't just scientific. Take, for example, a woman I worked with early in my career. I was her manager, and without exception, she would cry every time I gave her even the slightest critique or constructive feedback. She immediately went to a very dark place at even the insinuation that she needed to improve.

Let me be clear here: the problem wasn't that she cried. Sometimes, crying is an uncontrollable or necessary emotional response. Feeling yourself verging on tears and asking for a moment to collect yourself is completely acceptable. So is just letting it go and allowing the emotion to pass through you and run its course.

The problem was that she cried *every time*. No matter what.

And it's not just crying that makes giving feedback difficult. It's meeting other emotions in response to it—anger, denial, stone-cold silence, passive-aggressiveness, and blaming others. These and all the other counterproductive emotions I've encountered in myself and others make it very difficult to give and receive feedback. And that is a problem, because being able to accept and take action on useful feedback—especially if that feedback is that you need to improve—is a crucial part of your job.

It is not an option to not receive feedback, so we simply *have* to get better at it. And, in the case of the constant crier, I had to give her feedback on how she received feedback. After all, as her manager, *I* barely wanted to engage in feedback conversations with her, so I couldn't imagine how much feedback she wasn't getting from others who just wouldn't bother at all.

A few other things that come up with regards to feedback:

- ○ Power differentials exist, of course, and we are all wise to be aware of and respectful of them. But being respectful does not mean being silent. The truth is, we all need to receive feedback, and often. There is no need to create a different dialogue based on a person's position, as long as you are being respectful. Direct communication is always best.

○ Whether you are on the giving or receiving end, feedback is personal. Feedback includes evaluating ways that you do things, or those things themslves. If you are a person in a power position, it's OK to say aloud, "This might be hard for you to hear. I've spent a lot of time preparing this for that reason. If you need a minute, I understand that and am happy to give you that time." If you are in a subordinate position, it's OK to acknowledge emotions as they arise. Often, simply acknowledging that you're feeling angry or shocked or hurt does a lot to diffuse an outburst.

○ Many people suck at *all* feedback—even the positive kind! Truthfully, I get more frustrated with people who struggle to receive positive feedback than negative—and I gotta say, that happens with women I've worked with way more often than men. They do what I call "Thanking the Academy." Tell me if this sounds familiar:

> ○ *"Me? Oh, that project was so much work, so many people worked on it with me! I mean, really, it was actually so-and-so who did all of the data analytics. I was just the project manager. Ugh, this is so embarrassing!"*

STOP HAVING THE RIGHT CONVERSATION WITH THE WRONG PERSON

Lots of people—*lots*—do this. I have done it and, if I'm being honest, did it almost *exclusively* much earlier in my career. In a nutshell, it's giving the really great or tough feedback about someone's performance to anyone *but* that person. Sound familiar?

"Scott has been a pain in my ass lately. He shows up late to meetings, he misses important context early in the conversation, and, since he also has no shyness about sharing his opinions loudly, he sets everyone back another twenty minutes by sharing an opinion that is uninformed or misses what we've covered in his absence."

OK, maybe that's not *exactly* the right conversation (the *pain in the ass* part isn't super helpful), but the rest of that has some useful information.

FOR SCOTT.

If you're having that conversation with not-Scott (or several not-Scotts) you are guilty of having the right conversation with the wrong person. Scott needs to hear this feedback, not Sue. Not Jerry. Not Aidene. Not Kiran.

Scott.

While sitting down with someone else and troubleshooting or preparing for a conversation with Scott *is* a valuable exercise, that's not the same as lashing out at Scott to a not-Scott. So, when you feel the urge to unload about someone's behavior to someone who isn't the person in question, remind yourself: unless said unloading is going to enable and prepare you to have the right conversation with Scott, you're wasting time for the sole purpose of making yourself feel better—not improving Scott's performance or giving him useful insight into how to do so.

FOCUS MORE ON THE FEEDBACK, LESS ON THE SOURCE

Relationship dynamics clearly influence a person's ability to give and receive feedback. Let's go back to the person stopping you in the hall and saying they have that dreaded feedback for you. And it's legit, honest feedback—something you're doing is holding you back in some way, and once you hear and act on the feedback, you'll significantly improve your effectiveness at work and in life. Remember the example above with the salesperson and the boss, where I said if you have the trust and the history and the relationship, that direct approach might be fine? Let's take that a step further to illustrate how and why that works more clearly.

Let's say the person who pulls you aside in the hallway is Oprah. What your initial response be? (Mine would be "OMG OPRAH YESSSSSSSSS OPRAH!")

I'm guessing that your initial response would be incredibly receptive, too. SHE'S OPRAH, after all. She's the kind, gentle listener whose opinion can sway an entire nation. She gives feedback with love on soft couches, and you both cry it out and feel better in the end, right? I'm making an assumption here that you'd be more than happy to hear what she had to say and probably make changes based on her words.

Now, let's take the exact same scenario (feedback is legit, it's something you need to hear, life will improve, etc., etc.), but the someone who pulls you aside this time is Simon Cowell, the cranky-ass judge from *American Idol* (or *X-Factor* if you're a Brit!). There are no soft couches and cry-fests here, just direct, brutal snark. What would your initial response to him be?

If you're being honest, your response would be different. Probably significantly. Simon is known for being shrewd and confrontational, and no matter what, your defenses would most likely be way up. Even if he said the exact same thing as Oprah, you'd be questioning his intent and scrutinizing his motives.

In other words, you would be reacting to the person, not the feedback.

You will receive feedback from people you don't care for. But that is where the work of being a scientist of your own behavior comes in. You should be reacting to the feedback, every time. If the feedback isn't useful, by all means, disregard it. But if it is, you should be open to it, no matter who delivers it.

And speaking of delivery, think about yourself for a moment. Are you an Oprah or a Simon? How might your relationships with your peers impact their ability to receive feedback from you?

MAKE IT USEFUL

Just as your actions matter in terms of making your company better or worse every single day, so do your words. Before giving feedback, you need to ask yourself a very important question:

IS THIS FEEDBACK USEFUL?

Underline that shit. Circle it in red pen. Put it on a Post-it note and stick it on your computer, on your bathroom mirror, in your conference room. Dog-ear this page. Because all the other stuff we've covered in this chapter is really important and can help you get better, but the single most important thing—whether you're on the giving or receiving end of the feedback in question—is whether or not what you're sharing or receiving is useful.

If it is, you should give it. You should always give useful feedback in a timely, respectful way. That includes reflecting on and acknowledging your role in the situation you are giving feedback about. Pick off defenses you see arising in the other person. Take out anything that is unhelpful. Defuse what you know are trigger words. This is hard work, but just because it's hard doesn't mean you shouldn't give feedback. It does mean that you have ownership of your words.

And, of course—if the feedback you're receiving is useful, you should take it. I don't care how much you dislike or distrust or disrespect—or don't know at all—the person giving it to you. If you receive useful feedback and you ignore it because you don't like the person giving it to you—pardon the blunt feedback from *me*—you're being an idiot. You don't have to like Simon Cowell to know that he's regularly right, and you don't have to be his friend to say, "Thanks, that was useful," and then apply the feedback he gave. If it's useful, then use it.

Think back on some of the people in your life who have achieved success. I would be willing to bet that they are probably good or *very* good at giving and receiving feedback. If I think of people in my own career and life who have excelled, I cannot think of any who haven't, for the most part if not always, figured out how to control their knee-jerk emotional responses to criticism and take feedback for what it is: useful insight into how they can improve.

Feedback is part of your role, no matter what your role is. And while hearing feedback might be hard, *not* hearing feedback is worse.

And for real—if this is a skill you struggle with, prioritize getting better at it. Take *Crucial Conversations* if you have access to the class, and if you don't, get a copy of the book and encourage some friends or coworkers to join you in reading it and applying what you learn in it. I promise it'll change your life for the better, just like it changed mine.

MIRROR MOMENTS

1. If you had to, in one word, honestly describe your style when it comes to *giving* feedback, what would that word be (and would others agree)? How useful has that been for you and others?

2. If you had to, in one word, honestly describe your style when it comes to *receiving* feedback, what would that word be (and would others agree)? How useful has that been for you and others?

3. Who are the people you're *most* comfortable giving feedback to or receiving it from, and why?

4. Who are the people you're *least* comfortable giving feedback to or receiving it from, and why?

5. How frequently are you having the right conversation with the wrong person? Why?

MOVE TO ACTION MOMENTS

- You have a coworker who seems to nitpick the tiny details about *how* you get things done and also seems to under-appreciate *what* you get done. This has been going on for months.

- You've been given feedback that you know deep down is true, but you reacted badly when you received it and know that you have damaged your reputation in the eyes of the person who gave it to you.

- A boss's behavior toward you and another coworker has been bothering you. He regularly gives you feedback that comes across as hurtful and intended to make you feel bad, not to help you improve.

BUT WHAT ABOUT . . . !?

I've given some important feedback to someone, and they simply won't take it. It feels like we are at an impasse. It's really affecting our team, but I've done all the right things. What should I do?

First and foremost, an important lesson on feedback: just because you give someone feedback does not guarantee that they will take it to heart and change their behavior. After all, haven't you ever gotten feedback that you heard but disagreed with and ultimately disregarded? I certainly have.

If the person you've given feedback to doesn't change immediately, they either don't want to change their behavior and are making a conscious decision not to or they've done the thing you've called out for so long that change will be hard and may come slowly. If you believe that it's unwillingness to change, you have to decide how big a deal you want to make of it (e.g. escalating to their leadership chain) and then proceed accordingly. If you think it's because they either don't know that they're still doing the thing you don't want them to do or that it's hard for them to change, a quick "Hey, I wanted to follow up on our last conversation because I haven't seen any changes and this is still affecting the team. Is there something I can do to help make it easier?" can go a long way to helping someone adopt a new behavior without making it look like you are calling them an idiot for not doing so already.

My boss is terrible at giving feedback. I feel like she is always very indirect, and I'm constantly guessing what she means. I'm uncomfortable confronting her about it, though. What should I do?

In this case it's great if you can be the change you seek. For example, be specific about what you need feedback on, and take the first pass at giving it to yourself in their presence. Maybe you just gave a presentation and your boss was in the room. You can say something along the lines of, "I think that my presentation went well, but I'm not sure if I got my points across as clearly as I'd like. Specifically, I think I need better examples about the impact of others' decision-making processes on our project timelines. What do you think?" By priming the pump a bit with the specific nature of the feedback you seek, you're more likely to get meaningful input from others.

Of course, you can also give feedback about feedback. I know that sounds super dry and arduous, but say that your boss tried to give you feedback on that presentation and she fell short. You should tell her that, because she likely won't know that her feedback is unhelpful if you don't tell her. "I appreciate the feedback you gave me on the presentation, but I was hoping to get more specific about the slides on project planning and whether or not I made my point clearly. What do you think?" Assume that your boss wants to be helpful but needs a little nudge from you to hone in on the most useful points to discuss.

PART THREE

THREE

YOU AND ... YOU.

OK, since we've already covered so much material that focuses on you and your role in many scenarios, you might wonder why there's a section that is almost exclusively about you. And why it's the biggest of the three in this book.

If you haven't picked up on it yet, I'm a firm believer that you are the key to lots of things, not the least of which is your own success. The chapters in this section reflect the really deep self-reflection type of work that you can do primarily on your own. Since you are the only person whose career will be with you always, what you apply here will benefit you regardless of your company and your peers, because it will make you more like . . . you.

8 | The Chapter about Not Having Multiple Identities

Just after I left corporate America to start my own business and get deep into the process of writing this book, I had the opportunity to speak on a panel about race relations in the workplace. To set the scene, I was the most casually dressed (more on that later), and because of that, I loved the first question the moderator asked the panel:

"When you were a child, what impressions did you have of working in corporate America, and how did your parents or the people who raised you influence those impressions?"

The other speakers answered eloquently with stories about how their parents worked hard to provide for their families, demonstrated strong work ethics, etc. And then it got to me:

"I think the most important observation I can recall is that I believed that work was somewhere you went to be someone you weren't in 'real life.'"

The audience leaned in and seemed really into that answer, so I went on.

"I mean, look at me versus the rest of the people in this room. This isn't to disparage anyone here or the suits and dresses you're sporting, as I think you all look really great. But, much as I respect those of you who are, I'm not a suit-and-tie guy. There are probably lots of people in this room who, like me, dread putting on a suit and tie but, as I used to do, put them on because it's part of the game we have to play to get in the door. I saw my mom and dad do the same thing. My mom had to wear a uniform because she was a dental hygienist, and my dad had to put on suits and ties. And as soon as they got home from work, they ripped that off and put on 'real' clothes. So my observation was that going to 'work' meant going to a place that required you to put who you really were on the shelf for the majority of your weekdays so you could fit in, and you could live your 'real' life on evenings and weekends."

But how we dress is only one of the things that plays into who we are and how we show up to others—at work or elsewhere. Let's look at it from a broader—if fictional—perspective.

Allow me to introduce you to a coworker you might be familiar with. I'll call her Nita. Nita considers herself to be fairly masterful at maintaining multiple personalities, and for good reason. At home, she is partner and mother extraordinaire, baking with her kids on Sunday mornings and planning biweekly date nights with her spouse of seven years. She is a PTO volunteer, a Pinterest-worthy party planner, and very active politically.

At work, a career she has dedicated her life to, she blends in easily in most any situation. She can strategically negotiate budgets and can pull several different approaches out of her hat to get her way. She tries (often unsuccessfully, but still, it's cute) to trade pop-culture jokes with her younger coworkers because she thinks it's important that they see her as "cool." If she is in a meeting with senior management, she can easily code-switch back into the assertive, no-nonsense negotiator she realized she needed to be when she finished grad school. Then, she can move into another meeting where she sheds the persona of devil's advocate and simply nods her head in agreement with whoever is the most senior in the room.

Her daughter suffers from a rare disorder and her family passionately supports a charity benefitting that cause, something she is very vocal about on Facebook but has successfully kept hidden from her coworkers. She would never want them to think that her personal life is distracting her from her job requirements. "I'm a million different people!" she jokes when people ask her how she does it. "A regular chameleon. That's my secret to success."

I'm guessing you, or someone you know, can relate to Nita. She is a master shape-shifter and can easily conform to whatever role she needs to play. For any number of reasons, this is celebrated in our society. If you haven't figured it out by now, I'm here to tell you that Nita is not as successful as she thinks she is, and oftentimes, neither are we.

First off, let me give our fictional friend some much-deserved credit. The struggle of balancing work and life is real, and she's doing quite well. I can appreciate even if I can't relate to her desire to keep her personal life personal; anyone who has ever worked with someone who is constantly bringing personal drama into the workplace can appreciate that. The problem isn't that she is "wearing multiple hats." We are all complicated, unique individuals. The problem is that in becoming the "chameleon," she has also become untrustworthy.

Hear me out.

No one knows—including Nita—what version of Nita will be showing up to work on any given day. Is it Nita the hard-core negotiator? Is it Nita the millennial wannabe? Is it Nita the kind and gentle strategist? And while it might be commendable that she keeps her personal life personal, the fact remains that her family life is exceedingly important to her. Wouldn't her team understand her, her philosophies, and her priorities better if they were at least somewhat privy to that?

You might be having a visceral reaction at this point. Nita has done nothing wrong, and she doesn't owe an explanation of her personal life to the people she works with. You are right about that. But what I would argue about Nita, and probably about most everyone reading this book, is that while we have all at the very least done this shape-shifting unintentionally, we often do it consciously and strategically. We are spending valuable time at work—time we could be spending solving actual problems—being selective about how we present ourselves, in an effort to please people and stay comfortable.

Before I go any further, let me state for the record that this is not a chapter asking you and the people you work with to become best friends. Think of Michael Scott in *The Office* and how well that strategy worked for him. That is not required to happen, though I'd argue that it's only even possible to become friends with coworkers if they really know who you are. It's also not meant to ignore that there are very real obstacles to authentic expression—the sexism, racism, or homophobia of others, for example—that can make this really difficult to do.

What I *am* advocating for is an easing of the pressure that trying to blend in puts on all of us, especially when that pressure is something we take on ourselves without anybody asking us to. Whether you take baby steps or giant leaps, I believe it will be a huge relief to you to just be . . . you.

STOP TRYING TO BUILD A BRAND; BUILD A REPUTATION INSTEAD.

There has been a significant push over the last decade or so for everyone to "build a personal brand" for themselves.

YUCK.

Consider for a moment the definition of the word "brand" itself, courtesy of Merriam-Webster: *a class of goods identified by name as the product of a single firm or manufacturer.*

When I think about how I want to be perceived and how I want to influence or impact others, it's not as a class of goods or services. It's as a person who has skills, insights, humor, imperfections, passions, and goals. And lots of other things. Brands have none of those; they just have attributes. My heart skipped a joyful beat when Sheryl Sandberg, Facebook's COO, was asked about this and had a similarly strong reaction: "The reason it's not right is that products are marketed . . . but people are not that simple. We're not packaged. And when we are packaged, we are ineffective and inauthentic."

When I encounter people who are trying to build themselves a "brand" to put out into the world, I often see that effort coupled with really strange behavior. They become obsessed with what others think of them as a *product*, not as a *person*. They shift their focus away from self-awareness and self-reflection to fixate almost exclusively on how they are perceived, by whom, and to what end. While it's normal, fine, and even considerate to be concerned with how you come across to others, it's less fine if the reason you're interested in their perception is to perfect your ability to be a chameleon. To be inauthentic with them as a means to achieving an end. Doing so often leads you down the path of *more* shape-shifting in an effort to find what will be popular with even more people, all the while becoming less recognizable to more than one person at a time. While you might be building a "brand," you're also building confusion and skepticism. And most people can tell when they're being marketed to instead of having an authentic experience. This is as true for people as it is for laundry detergent.

For comparison purposes, here's how Merriam-Webster defines "reputation": *overall quality or character as seen or judged by people in general; recognition by other people of some characteristic or ability.*

See the difference?

I realize completely that you may be thinking this is just

semantics, but it isn't. People who focus on building a personal brand for themselves are trying to define how others see them by way of smart marketing, contorting themselves into "being" what that market demands. People who focus on building their reputations are trying to influence others to see them as their behavior shows them to really be. And telling the world how great you are at something is nothing like being able to actually show them that greatness.

And aren't you at least a little bit exhausted by people who are constantly telling you how awesome or perfect they are, even when you know better? Isn't it enough to be sorely misled by marketing that shows you a picture of a perfect burger only to unwrap an ugly mess when you actually buy it? Or to see yourself in the mirror after buying that Calvin Klein underwear and feel sad that it doesn't transform you into a bronzed god in a black-and-white beach scene?

I think it's bad enough that we let ourselves be misled by false advertising for a product we're considering buying. I can't play along with people who want to create the same type of smoke and mirrors about people.

SAY WHAT YOU MEAN

Another form of authenticity is visible or audible in the words that we use. Scrolling through Facebook and listening more intently to live conversations I can't help but overhear has reinforced for me how incredibly common it is for us to say things we don't really mean. The number of "literally"s used while not being literal (you're not *literally dead* if you're able to talk about being *literally dead*—or, for that matter, talk at all), the number of "OMG BEST THING EVER"s (last night may have been great, but was it really better than every other night ever experienced?), or the number of "We should totally get together soon!"s said by people who know that they have no intention of getting together—soon or not-so-soon. LOLs when not even a smirk has broken. It's a long list.

Now, think about this in a work setting. When someone asks you your opinion, listen carefully to how you respond. Are you so busy figuring out how to be nonconfrontational that you actually don't say anything meaningful? Are you so focused on nodding yes and making other people feel good or validated that you aren't actually listening to the problem and coming up with a creative solution?

I think we all tell ourselves that these little lies of language are harmless, but I don't believe that to be true. It gets harder and harder to actually know what the hell we're all talking about when we are so loose with shared meaning. And I think it makes it easier for people to be insincere, both when it doesn't matter much (describing an "epic" night out that was fun but wasn't going to be reported on CNN) and when it matters very much indeed (you're unreliable for the people counting on you because you didn't mean it when you said you'd be there for them).

This is a chapter about how living an authentic life, whatever that means to you, is an important piece of being a successful contributor to your company and team.

IMPOSTER SYNDROME

If you haven't figured it out already, we're all just kind of faking it. All of us, every day. Two psychologists back in 1978 coined the phrase "imposter syndrome" to describe the persistent fear of being exposed as a "fraud," or at the very least someone who isn't quite as smart as they might appear.

You have felt that way. I have felt that way. Bill Gates has, undoubtedly, felt that way. It's normal. And the data shows pretty clearly that the women reading this book are more prone to thinking this way than men.

The problem isn't that imposter syndrome exists but that we now live in a time where it's easy to let this fear of being discovered as less than perfect dictate how we live our lives. Social media can be a perfect enabler of this. Think of your social media accounts, assuming you have them. Sure, your LinkedIn profile isn't going to look exactly like your Facebook page. One is for business and one is for pleasure. But are they so different that they are essentially different people? Are you spending *any* amount of energy switching between the LinkedIn version of yourself that you let your coworkers see and the Facebook version that your friends and family get to know? If so, you are more than likely wasting valuable time. And for what? To stay comfortable and "safe"?

Think about your average day. Chances are, you are running from meeting to meeting, group to group, different audience to different audience. Then you go home, put on the "friends and family" hat, and become the person you think your friends and family need you to be. This is the reality of life for almost all of us. If you are spending even one minute between each of those activities shifting who you are to fit into the situation, that's several minutes per day.

Multiply that across an entire career, an entire lifetime, and that's a lot of wasted energy.

People who are in imposter-syndrome denial think that they are the Meryl Streep of managing multiple identities. You might think you are an incredible actor, but I'm here to tell you you're most probably not. You, with all your imperfections, will be found out for who you are. Nita, who so carefully dances around her team members, is bound to lose her temper at work, as she allows herself to do in certain company outside of work. When it happens, those team members who were used to working with an entirely different version of Nita are going to be shocked, hurt, and maybe even unwilling to take a risk with her again. Trust may be irreplaceably lost. And without trust in your team, how can you possibly work together to make a positive impact in your organization?

And all that work stress Nita takes home with her, the stress she so carefully hides from her spouse and children? That's going to come out, too. Maybe in large ways, maybe in small ways. The point is that when it does come out, when her loved ones *also* see her as someone who shifts and shapes into whatever situation she is in, there will be some trust lost in her by the people she loves most, too.

THE COMPLICATED TASK OF BEING YOURSELF

Let's say you're with me up until this point. *I get it! Be me! Unapologetically me! Don't hide, don't pretend to be perfect! I'm going to let my freak flag wave high and extend a big, fat middle finger to anyone who can't handle my authentic amazingness!*

Yeah . . . no.

Let's visit another important concept summed up beautifully by the author Brené Brown: authenticity is not an excuse to overshare. This is really important, so let's repeat it in bold: **authenticity is not an excuse to overshare.**

Take a moment to think about your favorite oversharer. You probably don't have to think too long. Maybe it's your elderly grandmother. Maybe it's a coworker who spends twenty minutes per day hopping from desk to desk complaining about his stream of bad dates. Maybe it's your boss, who hijacks at least a quarter of any meeting with a story about his politics or his lunch or whatever else pops into his stream of consciousness.

These people's oversharing behaviors are annoying. They are also not doing anything other than seeking the approval of others for being unabashedly themselves. That approval-seeking behavior is the exact opposite of true authenticity.

Part of making peace with your authentic self is being extraordinarily self-aware. Self-awareness comes in two steps:

the first is figuring out *you*, for all your strengths and weaknesses. The second is being courageous in that identity.

Figuring out who you are might be easy. If that's the case, you likely tend to live a fairly open life anyway, you don't have the tendency to overshare, and people, generally, seem to think you're OK. It won't be a huge leap for you to figure out how to quit code-switching from meeting to meeting, person to person.

If that is the case, great. But maybe there is a part of your authentic self that you keep private for a specific reason. Maybe your authentic self could be met with hostility. Maybe your authentic self in no way aligns with your company's values and mission. Maybe you are terrified that showing your true self in a meeting will get you fired. Maybe the idea of being exposed for who you really are brings you genuine fear.

Maybe all those fears are justified. But maybe they aren't.

Regardless, you are making a choice between courage and comfort. More specifically, you're choosing between having the courage to be yourself in spite of the risks and the comfort of being the person that other people are sure to accept because it's a role that they are familiar with and generally approve of.

No matter what is holding you back from being *you* in any situation, if you're choosing to be a less-true version of you, then you are choosing comfort. You are choosing not to rock the boat. You are also, I hate to say, choosing the path of wasted energy. If that is the path you choose, nothing I say in this chapter or book can change that decision for you. Just know that this decision to hide who you really are is impacting you and your team in all kinds of negative ways. And from a business perspective, one of the prices you pay for choosing this incessant shape-shifting is that neither you nor the people you work with will ever know your full potential—it's buried somewhere in version 37 of you.

At the same time, if you are ready to share the "real" you, be prepared to answer questions about it, because authenticity isn't an immediate guarantee of acceptance.

Just because you are showing your true self doesn't mean everyone will automatically or immediately (or ever!) understand you, and while you don't owe anyone an explanation of *why* you are who you are, you do need to have the self-awareness to know that your decision to be unreservedly *you* might raise an eyebrow or two. You might need to explain or even defend yourself or your behavior. We're all human beings, after all, juggling one unique personality with the next. Tensions might arise, and that is OK. That is real life. That is the price of admission that authenticity demands.

I've experienced this countless times in my own career. I mentioned earlier speaking on a panel where I was the most casually dressed member. That's pretty common for me, as I'm a pretty casual person. I have received plenty of shit over the years for my casual presentation. Plenty.

I've had bosses tell me that I would never get ahead if I didn't dress up more for my daily work. Conference organizers have fretted that I wouldn't be taken seriously if I didn't look as formal everyone else in the room. I even got sent back to a break room to "dress up" by one employer who was terrified that a customer would take me less seriously in handling his or her business because I was wearing a hooded sweatshirt on "casual" Friday. Apparently, I had made it "too casual" Friday. And without fail, before I speak or teach a class or write an article or even a book, people who see me assume that being in jeans means I'm less competent or unworthy of being taken seriously. There is, in most parts of the business world outside of the tech industry, a very conscious bias about people who dress casually for work.

But this "casual" aspect of me is part of my identity. If I were to be forced to wear a suit to each of my presentations or classes or meetings, my physical and mental discomfort would quite significantly impact my ability to do a good job.

Sure, you might be thinking. *That's easy for you to say. You worked in tech!*

And you're right about that. It's one of the reasons I chose to pursue my career in tech and not, for example, financial services. The dress code in almost every company outside of tech was a deal-breaker because it would force me to put on an appearance that didn't represent me.

That doesn't mean I can't or won't or shouldn't compromise, but I do it sparingly. It also doesn't mean that there aren't prices to pay. I don't accept offers to speak at events if I have to dress up too much because I couldn't imagine talking about my career—spent largely in jeans—while wearing a suit. It's not who I am. I work in and around tech companies because they, like me, value output and impact much more than presentation or pomp and circumstance. We've always been a good match like that.

I don't expect that everyone will accept this line of thinking, because they are not me. It just means being honest about and OK with the trade-offs if I compromise.

Figuring out who you are, being OK with who you are, and then putting into practice the delicate work of being authentically you is not easy work, nor is it necessarily meant to be. Each and every day, both personally and professionally, you will be met with challenges to living authentically. It might seem nearly impossible to change from corporate chameleon to authentic contributor, but the return on your investment into yourself is clear: shedding your multiple personalities is going to save you a ton of time and energy, and make you a better employee.

It's also going to make you a better human.

WORRY LESS ABOUT BEING INTERESTING, MORE ABOUT BEING INTERESTED

One of the things that I think has happened with the advent of social media and our "always-on" world of self-expression is that many of us—if not all of us, at one time or another—have moved away from being concerned about being interest*ed* as much as we are concerned with being interest*ing*.

In a social media context, think about it this way: how much do you spend posting about yourself (photos, updates about your daily life, major experiences, etc.) vs. scrolling through your feed and hearing about other people's experiences? Do you do more telling than asking? Are you more worried about watching a concert or filming it to prove to other people that you're there?

There's of course nothing wrong with wanting to tell people who matter to you what's going on in your life or wanting to talk or post about things that you care about. I'd be hypocritical if that were the point I was making, as I do both a lot. Hell, you're reading a book I wrote about my thoughts. That's not my point. What I'm saying is that if you're only allowing space for you to be the one sharing, your desire to be seen for you who you are has the potential to crowd out the ability for others to do the same. And more importantly, the more we focus on ourselves and our own stories, the more our empathy for and curiosity about the experiences and identities of others suffer.

Look, I've struggled with this myself. I was fortunate to have an opportunity to work with an exceptional executive coach, Thuy Sindell, who after several months of partnership could feel our mutual frustration at not being able to quite figure out what was holding me back in my career. I was well-liked, very capable at what I did, had lots of great ideas, and influenced the culture of my company on a daily basis. Yet there were some people I worked with who found either my behavior or just *me*—yikes—off-putting.

Yeah. Yikes.

But in one particular coaching session, she highlighted an example of me shutting someone else down with my behavior (being a little lecture-y in an internal group thread about the "right" and "wrong" ways to approach something.) I lost my shit and practically yelled, "TEACHING PEOPLE IS WHAT I AM PAID TO DO AT THIS FUCKING PLACE!" to which she got equally pissed and came back at me with:

"THAT DOESN'T MEAN YOU HAVE PERMISSION TO DO IT TWENTY-FOUR HOURS A DAY!"

In that moment, we both gasped and pearl-clutched and whatever else you do when some profound shit enters the room and introduces itself. There was a time and a place for me to offer up that type of expertise—in a classroom, primarily—because it was a place where other people wanted to hear from me or my experiences. But for everywhere else, I needed to be a hell of a lot more curious—and if I was going to just blaze them with brilliance, I should be a lot more understanding of the fact that being Mr. Teacher was something that required permission when I wasn't in front of a class. It was a hard lesson to learn, but one that serves me to this day.

It's not easy being as interested in others as ourselves, but it's certainly worth it. And it creates a virtuous cycle, I've found: the more interest I have in others—real, genuine interest, not that fake "How are you doing *please don't answer*!?" shit that poses as interest—the more I find common ground, mutual interest, and use for my own ideas or thoughts.

As I've said several times, the reason I'm encouraging you (OK, strongly encouraging you) to do this is not because it's easy to be yourself. It's difficult—especially when the people you really want to accept you don't or won't unless you change who you are for their benefit. But they're probably temporary figures in your life. You're going to be with you forever, and you'll sleep a lot more soundly knowing that you did the *real* you proud.

Also? Authenticity is contagious. When people see you being comfortable being you—the real you—it encourages them to be their authentic selves, too. And, after all, being that type of role model is what leadership is all about.

MIRROR MOMENTS

1. What pieces of your identity are you obscuring at work, and what real or perceived benefits are you realizing for doing so?

2. Imagine the best-case scenario you would face if your co-workers knew more about you as a human being. What benefits could you realize having someone know more about your authentic self?

3. What trade-offs have you accepted that you are not really comfortable with, and what might you have to give up in order to live more authentically?

4. What is an instance you have purposely been inauthentic in order to please others or achieve success because you

felt that being your authentic self would have not been as effective? Why?

MOVE TO ACTION MOMENTS

- A coworker regularly makes comments about LGBT people that, while probably not intended to be harmful, reinforce stereotypes and make it easier for you to justify hiding your sexual orientation at work.

- You are an avid gamer (lover of video games, for you nongamers out there) and think that there are probably others in your company. But despite there being lots of interest groups for other employee interests, you've never tried to set up one that caters to this interest.

- You've brought so much of your personal life into work that you feel a bit overexposed. You share really personal details about your life with your coworker Facebook friends and you've heard indirectly that a few of these coworkers now feel uncomfortable around you because of this intimate knowledge.

BUT WHAT ABOUT . . . !?

Being myself is a lot harder than I thought it was going to be. I find myself reverting to old habits when I feel vulnerable. What should I do?

First and foremost, you have to recognize that the source of that discomfort and vulnerability is largely the inner dialogue in your own head. Most people are paying *far* too much attention to themselves and their own shit to be terribly concerned with you and yours. This is one of those things that is both liberating and frustrating: we don't want people to pay too much attention to us because it can make us feel self-conscious, but we also don't want them to pay *no* attention to us because it can feel like they're judging us.

For almost every permutation of humanity, there are at least several people who can relate to you as you are, and the best advice I give people is to seek out others who can relate, have empathy, and give advice and not to take too seriously the validation of others as a metric for success in being authentic. You are the one who has to live with you and care most about you, and on the days where doing so is hard, know that everyone else probably feels the same way about themselves.

I am not sure how to figure out who I am. I mean, I know who I am. But I don't know who I really am. You know?

Welcome to being alive. Come on in, the water's fine.

9 | The Chapter about Being Proudly Strong

On May 24, 2011, I took a sick day. It wasn't just any old day—it was the day of the final episode of *The Oprah Winfrey Show*, and I wasn't going to miss it for anything. Oprah didn't disappoint. Much of the message of that last show focused on identifying and then pursuing your purpose, something I was struggling to do, especially just one month into my tenure at Facebook.

Speaking about the twenty-five years spent on her record-shattering talk show: "What I know for sure from this experience with you is that we are all called. Everybody has a calling, and your real job in life is to figure out what that is and get about the business of doing it. Every time we have seen a person on this stage who is a success in their life, they spoke of the job, and they spoke of the juice that they receive from doing what they knew they were meant to be doing. We saw it in the volunteers who rocked abandoned babies in Atlanta. We saw it every time Tina Turner, Celine, Bocelli, or Lady Gaga lit up the stage with their passion. Because that is what a calling is. It lights you up and it lets you know that you are exactly where you're supposed to be, doing exactly what you're supposed to be doing. And that is what I want for all of you and hope that you will take from this show. To live from the heart of yourself.

You have to make a living; I understand that. But you also have to know what sparks the light in you so that you, in your own way, can illuminate the world."

Interestingly, if you google quotes or concepts from that final show that people really latched on to, this doesn't show up. The ones about "aha moments" and "live from the heart of yourself" and the other touchy-feely themes she's known for (and fine, I love a few of them too) got all the press that this one didn't. But my "aha moment" that day was when I realized that what Oprah was talking about was a concept I'd started researching and almost immediately started teaching at Facebook—playing to your strengths.

It might sound counterintuitive given what I do for a living, but the thing I've struggled with most is understanding, identifying, leveraging, and prioritizing my strengths. I've found, both in my own experience and in helping to manage and teach others, that while it is easy to list off all of the things at which we suck, being clear and articulate about our strengths is hard as hell. This is probably due to a million reasons, not the least of which being that we—well, many of us—live in a world where it is far more socially acceptable to obsess about and telegraph our weaknesses to others. If you think about the headlines you see in a grocery store magazine rack, most of them are probably telling you how deficient you are and how they hold the secrets to fixing all that is wrong with you. For example: as of this writing, a search for "self help" on Amazon returns 693,864 results, and many of the books and resources and fad diets and ridiculous exercise plans and supplements are there to help you identify or fix where you're broken and how to improve everything that's wrong with you. It's worth noting, though, that the backlash to all of this ridiculous "fix what is wrong with you!" content out there is in many ways just as dangerous to our thinking, even if it is more fun. The number one result of all of those was Mark Manson's *The Subtle Art of Not Giving a F*ck: A Counterintuitive Approach to Living a Good Life*—a book I very much enjoyed, though a society filled with people who really don't care about what others think about them isn't really any more sustainable than one paralyzed by it.

So as Oprah said on that last show and as Marcus Buckingham—a gentleman I've referred to several times in this book—concurs, let's shift our thinking more toward this: "A strength is an activity that makes you feel strong." It's not just an activity at which you excel but for which you also have passion. Buckingham goes on to say, "A strength is not just what you're good at any more than a weakness is just what you're bad at"—in other words, ability is half of the equation and passion is the other part.

These concepts aren't new or even particularly radical—indeed, *First, Break All the Rules* was first published in the late nineties, and its claims that playing to strengths matters more than everything else as far as impact, fulfillment, job satisfaction, and retention are concerned unfortunately failed to turn the world upside-down. Even Oprah's own love letter to pursuing purpose got swallowed up by the other things she covered on that show. I've come to believe that this is because we think following our purpose is common sense and common practice, and it just isn't. Most people believe, as I did, strengths and abilities to be interchangeable, but they are not.

For example—I'm really good at finance and managing budgets. I have had many instances in my career where, thinking that being a good team player was the most important thing I could do, I volunteered to do things that I was good at but really, really didn't enjoy. Finance. Spreadsheets. Teaching content that I didn't care for. Running meetings. I didn't take those things on because they were my strengths; I took them on because I was good at them and I thought that doing what I was good at was the secret to success (and, more importantly, to having impact).

But it wasn't. It really wasn't. It was the "secret" to getting things done at high personal cost. To doing work that was not only unfulfilling but also puzzling because all external indicators pointed to my being successful. In all of these cases, I ended up quitting the jobs where I had been successful but unhappy, impactful but unfulfilled, and pointed the finger of blame for my misery at everyone else—my managers, my peers who wouldn't take their share of the shitty work, my employers, the economy that necessitated so many unpleasant trade-offs—instead of taking ownership for my decisions to take on work that played to my ability but not my passion.

In reality, there is a very long list of things that we're bad at and a very short list of areas where we excel, and if you employ old-school thinking about growth and opportunity, you probably believe that you're going to grow the most if you focus on the longer list more than the shorter one. And you'd be wrong. You don't have to believe me or believe Marcus (but you should—we're right, I promise), you just need to pay attention to your own emotional responses at work.

Indeed, there are likely many things that you'll need to become at least moderately competent at if you don't want them to derail you in your pursuit of your strengths. Every engineer that wants to grow their ability to influence others most likely needs to also learn to articulate his or her ideas in groups of people, so being bad at presenting ideas is a deal-breaker in the long-term. But trying to become the best public speaker in the world is probably going to be a waste of time. Getting good enough is probably, well, good enough, because presenting ideas is most likely a complementary activity for an engineer, not a primary one.

Let's give this a try: maybe none of you reading this will never be as good as I am at owning a room. After all, I'm better at it than most people.

You probably just re-read that sentence two or three times and thought, "Wow, that wasn't even a humblebrag, it was full-on." And you're wrong—it wasn't. I'm really happy that I can walk into just about any room and connect in a real and meaningful way with almost everyone. It is one of the few things in the world that I really love doing and that I'm better at than most people. After all, for many people, public speaking precedes dying on the list of things that terrify them and that they're bad at doing. But for me, it's the best thing in the world. And yet when I say that out loud or put it in writing, most people will likely think I'm full of myself for doing so. We are conditioned to believe that owning what we excel at is equal to being a jerk. Why?

The reason I can say that sentence at all and tell you that I'm not bragging is that I immediately follow it up with the fact that I suck at way more things than I excel at and always will. I'd be a terrible software engineer, I hate the thought of selling anything even though I'm kind of good at it, and even though I love cooking I'll never be a master chef. Did you have to re-read that to believe I'd said it? Probably not—we're all brought up to believe that this type of brutal honesty about our abilities is OK because it makes us fit in more than it makes us stand out. Well, I don't know what else to say but . . . fuck that.

I want to stand out. I want everyone to stand out. Not for everything, and not in the "everyone gets a trophy" or "Look at me, damnit!" kind of way—that type of false spotlight only shines on your weaknesses in the end, because nobody is good at everything. But I want to stand out for what I'm great at, and I want to be surrounded by people who stand out for what *they're* great at. It's why I do the work I do and why I'm great at it—it's on the very short list of reasons I was born.

There are, of course, trade-offs. Sometimes we desperately want to be great at things that we'll just never master, and it's painful to accept those shortcomings—especially if we compare our weaknesses to others' strengths. More often, other people desperately want us to be great at something—usually more for their own benefit than for ours—and we don't want to disappoint people. Or ourselves. The day my life and career took off was the day I let all that go, and the trade-offs (the occasional disappointment, the sometimes heavy or brutal reminders of my limits) are offset by the awesome feeling of spending so little time on shit I don't care about or for which I possess little or no talent.

In the end, this is obviously about way more than just owning a room. It's about who I am and what I'm great at; it's about who you are and what *you're* great at; and it's about the immense amount of courage and tenacity it takes not to lose focus on those things in a world where we are surrounded by people who are trying to fit in and stand out at the same time. I said that I was motivated by the questions—I was. To share this. To help more people find the intersection of their skills, the things they are passionate about, and their ability to use those things to make a difference in the world.

You may be asking yourself—"What does this have to do with organizational culture?" Well, simple: we're all happier, more productive, more impactful, and more fulfilled when we and the people around us are doing work that plays to our strengths. And a company filled with people optimized to do their best, most fulfilling work is a company that will win.

Marcus's research confirms it, the work we did internally at Facebook confirms it, but perhaps most importantly, common sense confirms it. If you want to be a culture leader in your company, you have to know what you are better at than most people—the reason you're really there—and do as much of it in as visible a way as possible. This doesn't mean bragging about how great you are all the time; we all despise that behavior. But it does mean doing the work to identify your biggest strengths and the means to leverage them to impact the people and work around you. It means talking openly about what drives you and what demotivates and drains you. It means paying attention to emotions—something many of us have to learn to be comfortable doing in life, let alone at work—because how we feel about our work is as important a driver of long-term performance as our ability to do the work.

It also, in many ways, requires a healthy suspension of judgment. One of the things that unfortunately but invariably results from a strengths-based focus is the temptation to judge work as "unworthy" if we personally don't love it or to judge ourselves and become insecure about loving something that isn't popular with others. But a little reflection kills this line of thinking—after all, I'm incredibly grateful for the people in my life and in my work who love doing the things that I can't or don't want to do. It is their passion for the things that drain me that enables me to focus on what I love, because the things I don't love still need to get done. Someone needs to do the spreadsheet. Someone needs to run the meeting. That someone just doesn't need to be me—and everything you and I hate doing is almost sure to be beloved and meaningful to someone else.

As silly as it may sound, it's important here to get comfortable saying out loud, "I really love doing [activity]," because being able to articulate it is the first step to letting others know to come to you for that work. It's equally important to get comfortable saying out loud, "I really despise doing [activity]," because if you don't, people will probably continue asking you to do it—especially if you're good at it or if you've done it in the past and never said anything about it being a drain on your motivation or your love for the rest of your job.

Is this risky? Sure. But being a leader is always about putting yourself out there in ways that will motivate and inspire others to follow suit, and this is one of the areas where you may have the biggest impact on your culture.

So yeah. Strengths. What are yours?

P.S. I didn't get here on my own. The work of Marcus Buckingham on strengths, Steven Smith on Egonomics *("I'm Brilliant and I'm Not" is from that amazing book), and Joseph Grenny and crew on* Crucial Conversations *are pieces of writing that changed my life. Will they change yours? I can't say for sure, but I'd sure recommend giving them a shot.*

MIRROR MOMENTS

1. If you had to describe your perfect day at work, what would you spend it doing? (*Note: this is also my very favorite question to ask candidates in job interviews.*)

2. If you're in a role that you're great at but that you don't enjoy, why have you stayed in the role? Asked another way: What benefit are you realizing from doing work that drains you?

3. What would moving into work that played more to both your ability and your passion look like? What additional trade-offs might you have to accept in order to do that?

MOVE TO ACTION MOMENTS

- A leader you respect and want to work with comes to you for help on a project. You're excited until you find out the work that is needed is something you absolutely hate doing but do very well.

- There's a new position posted in your department and you're dying to apply for it. It hits everything you're passionate about, but also has a handful of qualifications on it that you don't feel you meet . . . yet.

- You've been in a role for two years that used to really engage and challenge you, but you're burned out. You have considered quitting a number of times, especially in the last month or two, but the rewards (hint: they're also called "money" and "bonus") are *amazing*.

BUT WHAT ABOUT . . . !?

I know what I'm good at, but it's not what I have the most expe-

rience doing. I can't seem to get myself into a position where I can really showcase my strengths. What should I do?

The first thing you need to do is ask yourself how you got to that point. If you accepted roles because you had to (you needed the money desperately, maybe) or because you'd never really considered passion an important part of your work, own that role. You may be in the wrong role, and that is probably mostly your fault #realtalk.

The good news is that you can make changes! If your current role has room in it for you to do more work that plays to your ability *and* your passion, great! Take a stab at articulating what that might look like and ask your manager if they are willing to go over it with you and, if you agree, make some tweaks to your set of responsibilities. If your current role really needs you to just get the stuff done you were hired to do, you have to decide how long that will be OK for you. If a change is needed, you'll also need to figure out how you'll go about doing it in a way that keeps your bills paid but your options open.

I have an employee who sees his strengths as one thing, but I see his strengths as something different. What should I do?

Have you ever watched an episode of *American Idol*? Have you ever seen contestants who, in the early parts of each season, are ready to take America by storm with their vocal prowess?

Did you watch the whole two-minute bios on this people, get invested in their success, and then hear, when they opened their mouth to sing, a horror upon your ears like no other?

Me too. I used to scream at my TV—"Why don't any of your friends or family love you enough to have prevented this atrocity!?"

In reality, it can be really hard to say "Yeah, this isn't really you." Especially if the person thinks they're great. But ultimately, remember, strengths are not for us to define for others; performance, however, is. And performance is far less subjective than an opinion on either side, so if you have someone deep in denial about their strengths, shift the conversation to their ability to perform—especially compared to others who are demonstrably badass at the same or similar skills.

And, if applicable, encourage them to take up karaoke.

10 | The Chapter about What to Do When You're Scared Shitless

Facebook has become well-known for its red-letter posters around campus, the most popular of which reads, "What Would You Do if You Weren't Afraid?" When people really stopped to ponder this question, the responses I heard were more often than not something I like to call "superhero responses."

"I'd solve world hunger!"

"I'd quit my job and sail around the world!"

"I'd give a TED talk!"

Sure.

I have a complicated relationship with this poster. On one hand, it inspires some really good conversations. It makes people think, and thinking is good. Thinking about what holds us back is especially good.

On the other hand, I have rarely heard people answer that question with something a bit smaller but more real-life. Something they have total control over, right at that moment. Something like:

"I'd tell my boss I'm unhappy in my role and want to make a change."

"I'd admit that I don't know exactly what I'm doing and that I need some help."

"I would put in a transfer to a different office, something I've always dreamed of doing."

If it were up to me, the poster would read differently. It would ask a question that really requires some serious reflection:

What will you do when you are afraid?

The answer to that question might be difficult to answer, and yet I would argue that it will set the course of your entire career.

So let's get to work.

THE SCIENCE OF FEAR

We've already established in the chapter about feedback that when a person is in a heightened emotional state, they are likely to make their worst and most self-sabotaging decisions, both personally and professionally. Fear, of course, is an emotional state—probably the largest, most dominant emotional state when it comes to bad decision-making. So it's important to know exactly what you fear, why you fear it, and what you are willing to do about it.

People are always happy to joke about their ridiculous phobia around [insert random thing here]. Your fear of clowns would be called an irrational fear, but you probably have other, more secretive irrational fears. Flying, for example. Or moving. Or starting over in a new career. These fears can be large or small, justified or unjustified, but they are there. What makes them irrational is that you *know* there is a much higher likelihood you'll die in the car on the way to the airport than on the plane ride itself, but despite that, you are still afraid of flying.

You probably have many fears that are seen as rational, if for no other reason than that they are shared by so many others. A fear of public speaking, for example. A fear brought on by a traumatic experience. A fear of taking on a new project. These fears are "rational" in that they are more personal to you. There are no scientific facts that can make you feel less shaky when you are shared shitless before you present in front of a crowd. There is no way that a statistic about aggression in dogs will take away a previous experience of being bitten by one. You can rationalize, personalize, and therefore be driven by these fears because you have personal experience with them.

The point of this chapter is not to take those fears away or to make any type of value judgement on you for having them in the first place. That is a job for you and your therapist. But I do think that managing the fears that tend to sabotage us at work is essential to our success in our companies.

Since you can't manage what you don't understand, now is the time to reflect on some of your rational and irrational fears, particularly as they relate to your work.

FEAR AS A CHOSEN STATE

It is easy for someone who does not share your fear to give sweeping generalizations about how to get rid of it. It's also easy to talk yourself out of dealing with your fears. I mean, one more day avoiding [insert scary task here] isn't going to kill anyone, right?

Ironically, it is that exact same hyperbolic talk that is going to get you out of being dominated by your fear and into actively managing it. But more on that later.

Exposure therapy is often a go-to method for psychologists who work with people dealing with things like anxiety, fear, phobias, and even PTSD. The idea is simple: you get over what you fear by being safely exposed to it, over time and in gradually increasing doses, while simultaneously being allowed to feel and work through the emotions that arise and exert your power over them. This is certainly true at work, too: the more you present, for example, the more comfortable you will be presenting. Fears diminish significantly or go away completely when you realize there is really nothing to fear in the first place.

I can honestly say there is very little I fear, both personally and professionally. Have I somehow been blessed with something superior to anyone else? Do I have some sort of psychological disposition to be fearless? Of course not. I do have fears, just like everyone else. The main difference is that when something is scary to me, I negotiate myself into the logical reasons for doing it instead of giving in to all of my fear-based justifications for turning and running away.

In other words, most of the time when something is scary to me, the idea of *not* doing the thing is much worse than the fear of doing it. Kids these days call it FOMO, or fear of missing out. When I have FOMO, I do the thing. I choose to do the thing.

When I was tasked with helping to create a course on

managing unconscious biases for Facebook, I have to admit that I was definitely afraid of failing. It was a huge task, a program on an incredibly important topic on which I possessed no significant expertise. Getting it right was important to me not only professionally but also personally. It was a high-priority, high-visibility project that we ultimately released to the entire planet, so the stakes were high. It was a project that focused on subject matter that people ran screaming from. I'd have to make myself and other people talk about something they found difficult.

In other words, there were lots of things that could go wrong, ruin my career, etc.

Enter the negotiation. What were the risks of not doing it? Without my instructional design expertise present, we could have gotten it wrong. Sure, I was no expert on bias, but I *was* an expert on learning. If that expertise was missing from the process, a lot of great content could be taught in a really unhelpful way and my company could suffer. That would hurt me, too.

I also couldn't stomach the thought of not doing the program just because other organizations had struggled to get it right or because we thought it was too hard. God knows I've seen *so many* companies shy away from the harder content and conversations because they thought that if it wasn't perfect, it wasn't going to work.

If you haven't noticed, I made the fear of not doing it about bigger, "us" things instead of making them about me.

My personal fears took a back seat to my fears about what might happen to a much larger group of people if we didn't do this well. And so I did the work, and it turned out to be one of the most profound experiences of not only my career but also my life. And the accomplishment meant an immense amount more to me because, while I had initially hesitated, I ultimately pushed through the fear and did it anyway.

Look, I can't say anything to guarantee your choices will be the right ones. No one can. What I can tell you is that living in a state of paralyzing fear is, ultimately, a choice you make. In the workplace, when you are tasked with something hard and your first instinct is to shirk away from it, you are giving into fear.

And that has far-reaching ramifications.

HOW FEAR-MENTALITY AFFECTS YOUR WORK

Let's go back to that situation I just brought up about being tasked to create a course on unconscious bias. Sure, I had plenty of corporate training experience, but creating this new program about a subject matter I wasn't familiar with was daunting. I had two choices: say yes or say no.

I said yes. And while the learning curve was steep and the stakes were really high, doing this project opened innumerable doors for me, career-wise. Would I have enjoyed the same successes without taking that risk? Definitely not.

Now, let's pretend I said no. Or worse, I sat around spinning in my own head, unable to make up my mind. What message would that have sent to my leadership team? Go back to what was asked of me and my fellow new hires on our first day at Facebook, the question everyone reading this book should be asking: "Why the fuck did we hire you?" I would have been sending a clear message to the people that mattered that I really didn't know *why* I was there in the first place.

Our behavior, more than anything else, has the ability to make or break our careers. The hard things we face aren't going away. In fact, they are going to keep coming. Ultimately, someone is going to figure out how to solve them, and in so doing, they will all but guarantee that other and likely bigger opportunities are going to go to the people who are willing to put the fear of failure aside and actually do the thing. As Sheryl is famous for saying: "The future belongs to those who are willing to get their hands dirty."

In the world of high tech, we talk a lot about risk and how we aspire to reward risk-taking. We also know that not all risks pay off. Silicon Valley is littered with the ghosts of bad risks, and nobody should ever take a risk that they know to be foolish. But when you look at why risk is valued more in tech than anywhere else, it's because none of the steep changes in technology would have happened by moving slowly or safely through problems or opportunities. Ultimately, a risk-taker is seen first and foremost as a doer, and we all like doers.

And if you're not a doer, you won't get ahead. The person who's willing to do the hard stuff, without a doubt, will achieve more professional and personal success.

FOCUSING ON OUTCOME

So we've established that fear is a part of life, and it is not an option to live without it. It is, however, an option to manage it successfully. But how?

In my experience, it's fairly simple. You play the "worst-case scenario" game. Here's how it works. You express your fear as well as the worst-case scenario around that fear.

I'm talking the worst of the worst-case scenarios. You die.

I've done this with people many times over my career. "Yes," I'll say. "If you take that new role, you will definitely die."

"Haha," the employee will say. "I won't die."

"Oh yes," I'll insist. "You will definitely die."

"I will not die!"

"OK, so then it isn't going to kill you, what is the *actual* worst-case scenario?"

After they are done laughing at the absurdity of that response, though, they do tend to understand my point: if something isn't going to kill you, maybe the outcome won't be so impossible to manage, even if it's not a great one.

Ultimately, this exercise helps people open up a bit (to me, yes, but more importantly to themselves) about what it is they actually fear. Obviously, a project, a public speaking opportunity, or a difficult conversation with someone is almost certainly not going to kill you. For the most part, the fears that prevent people from taking risks at work break out into two main camps: fear that they will fail and fear that they will lose the confidence of others. Or, worst of all, there's the fear of not being liked; by this point you know how I feel about letting *that* dictate your career.

The way to overcome fear, or at the very least manage it, is to focus on the possible outcomes. Play the "worst-case scenario" game, but instead of throwing yourself into ridiculous hyperbole, focus on the things that you are actually afraid of, and the outcome of either doing or not doing a thing that seems scary.

For example, "I have to _____. It is scary to me because _____."

And, since inertia is just a different, more terrible way of saying no to the call to action, you will need to make a choice between action and inaction, both of which have consequences. Quite simply, you'll need to make a list that would look something like this:

Possible outcomes of me doing the thing	Possible outcomes of me not doing the thing

This isn't to say that you will always or should always choose to take a risk, of course. There will be plenty of times when you will carefully negotiate risk versus benefit, both personally and professionally, and realize that the best answer to the call to action is "no." But I want that answer to come from a place of really understanding outcomes instead of being dictated from a place of fear.

OVERCOMING FEAR

Obviously, overcoming fear is ongoing work. It is a choice you will make daily, both in your personal and professional life. This work isn't easy, but it's absolutely critical to your success.

The people I know who manage fear best are the people who voice their fears as they arise. "This is daunting AF!" they might say when given a huge task. " . . . And here is why." In doing so, they are doing a *number* of things that good leaders do. First, they're being open and honest. Second, they're admitting that they're human beings (something currently labeled as "vulnerability" but I prefer to call "being real") because all human beings have fears. They are also showing trust in others, because admitting a fear shows others that we see them as allies who can help us to understand the bigger picture or just see it a bit differently. A good manager will hear their employee voice a legitimate fear and help them to see positive outcomes they might not be able to think of on their own. A decision can then be made from a place of understanding and data rather than being based solely on an often irrational emotion.

Steve Jobs is quoted as saying, "Envy is a powerful motivator and a weak navigator." He was talking about his business, of course, but I actually think this applies to fear as well. It can, indeed, sometimes be a good motivator or navigator—after all, fearing tigers will help navigate you away from jumping into a ring with one. But approximately 0 percent of the "scary" scenarios we face in our daily lives are equivalent in any way to getting into a ring with a tiger, tempting as it may be to act like it.

At the heart of this entire book is the idea that your life is your own *Choose Your Own Adventure* book. And at the heart of *that* idea is that when you look at yourself in the mirror, when you reflect on your career as well as your personal life, you will need to reckon with only yourself about whether or not you've led a happy and fulfilled life.

Managing fear is the first step toward that fulfillment.

MIRROR MOMENTS

1. What is the actual worst-case scenario associated with action [risk] and what might the consequences be if it happens?

2. Who do you know who has successfully navigated this risk and could give you some pointers or advice on how to achieve a similar outcome? (Hint: one surefire way is to tell people you trust the things you're afraid of and watch the advice and support and "OMG me too!"s pour in.)

3. What will the consequences of not taking the risk be, and how will you see yourself differently if you let the opportunity to step up pass you by?

4. What would you do if you weren't afraid, and what will you do when you *are*?

MOVE TO ACTION MOMENTS

○ You have worked out a clear solution to a big problem, but it's not your known (by others) area of expertise and a much more experienced person caused the problem in the first place.

○ Giving presentations gives you palpitations and you already bombed one last year. There's a huge promotion up for grabs and you're ready in every other way, but the additional responsibility will come with new requirements for presenting to large groups.

○ A project you're working on is going sideways and you know that, if you don't get some help fast, things are going to fall apart. The other people on your team who are *not* working on the project are also stretched thin and your boss has made it clear that budgets are tight.

BUT WHAT ABOUT . . . !?

I took a risk and it blew up in my face. I am embarrassed and ashamed of the result. I've admitted fault and reflected on what I could have done better. What should I do to get over it?

Bear with me, because you might hate me a bit for this answer: the best thing you can do is one more scary thing—admit what happened to the people who are impacted by it. For one, they probably already know that you fucked up, so admitting it isn't going to rock their worlds. But while we tend to really hate people who make messes and then deny their role or fail to take any part in cleaning them up, we *love* people who acknowledge their humanity—and being human involves a super-healthy amount of fucking up—and seek out help.

It's important to reflect—what were you trying to accomplish, what do you think went wrong, why do you think (or know, if you really know) it went wrong, and what have you learned from it? This amount of self-awareness and willingness to figure out why things went the way they did will almost always get you a golden ticket to "Help Me Fix This Shit"-ville. They will also help you get over it, and you should—most failures really don't matter that much in the grand scheme of things, especially if you learn enough from them to not repeat the failure again.

My coworkers are constantly asking me to take risks I'm not comfortable taking. It's not that I'm afraid; it's that I'm actively choosing to say no. How do I make sure people respect my choices, even when the choice is no?

You can't have it both ways. If you're not comfortable doing so, you're choosing to say no, but that choice might be based in fear and likely is. You might need to learn new skills or rely on others more than you do when doing things that are in your comfort zone, but those are hardly reasons to avoid taking risks. Again—be transparent about what concerns you and the trade-offs you think you may need to make to make things work. If the answer is ultimately still no, just explain your thinking. Most of the time when people don't respect your choices it's not because they're the wrong choices, it's that others don't understand why you're making them.

11 | The Chapter about Managing Your Unconscious Biases

One of the first things that any organization does before they've even hired you is start exposing you to their biases. You do the same in return. Organizational values are a reflection of a company's biases. Where a company locates itself is a reflection of its biases. How the people at the company dress is a reflection of its biases. And, of course, the people that a company hires or doesn't hire are a reflection of its biases.

And if you're thinking I'm saying all of that to be critical of them, you're wrong. Biases can be incredibly useful, after all. Imagine you work in a tech company, as I have for most of my career. Many tech companies, including Facebook and Microsoft and Apple and Dropbox and Uber and so on, have biases for advancing the world via technology. That bias or belief that technology can and should help make our lives easier, longer, or happier has resulted in incredibly useful (and yes, some not-so-useful) breakthroughs in the last century.

I'll give you a more specific example: one of Facebook's most important organizational values, in my experience, is its bias for moving quickly. The value itself was simple: move fast. That meant that when push came to shove, we placed a higher value on decisions that erred on the side of more speed, not less. We valued behavior that helped projects and decisions to not get bogged down in bureaucracy, second-guessing, or, god forbid, a million meetings. We rewarded behavior that optimized for speed.

Another example: there's a very visible bias in the tech industry for being more casual and more like the version of yourself you are outside of work. This type of authenticity is so prevalent and something I believe in so vehemently that I wrote a chapter on it in this very book. If you wonder how strong this bias is, go for a job interview at a tech company and show up in a three-piece suit. It's not necessarily a deal-breaker, but I can virtually guarantee that someone will comment on you sticking out because of what you're wearing. Indeed, the few times I wore anything that wasn't essentially jeans, a T-shirt, and a hoodie to work—my standard uniform—people would whisper, "What's up? You interviewing somewhere?"

All of this is to say that organizations and the people in them have lots of biases, they celebrate those biases in the form of stated values and posters and the like, and all of those things can help them shape their cultures in really meaningful and healthy ways.

The flip side of these helpful and useful biases is that our useful, conscious biases are far fewer in number and often in strength than our unconscious biases. That's where we and the companies we work for face almost certain trouble unless we (a) know them and (b) learn how to correct for them before they sabotage us. So this chapter is not a celebration of our conscious biases and values, beliefs that in many ways make us great. It's about understanding and acknowledging all of the harmful shit that goes on in our brains that can "help" us—often without our knowledge or consent—create environments we don't want, alienate people we do want, and flail helplessly when trying to figure out who's to blame for these results we neither desire nor understand.

Before we jump in, it's worth spelling out specifically what the business case for becoming aware of your own biases is, since it has, for some reason I can't fathom, become a point of contention between those who believe that it is a waste of time and those who do not.

There are specific types of bias that tend to become more prevalent, and therefore more institutionally ingrained, the larger an organization becomes. In the United States and many other parts of the world, those biases disproportionately and negatively impact women and underrepresented minorities. If you are a woman and/or person of color in the US, nothing about that statement shocks you, but if you're a white male, it might be hard to stomach. While there are myriad different types of bias out there, fueled by our own imaginations and unique experiences, ample research has proven the very real biases that exist on a large scale and how they manifest themselves. For a really interesting look into this, I highly recommend reading *Blindspot: Hidden Biases of Good People* by Anthony Greenwald and Mahzarin Banaji.

Some really high-level examples: research shows that US companies hire whites and men and especially white men based on potential while we hire women and/or people of color based on proven experience. We dislike women who have children and work, but admire men who do the same.

OUCH. That's hard to admit.

Take a deep breath, though. In many cases, we do these things subconsciously. Nobody (I hope!) looks at a resume and tells themselves, "Ah, this candidate has a Black-sounding name. I hope he has eight more years of experience than the white candidate I just interviewed if he wants me to consider him for the role!" Or, "Sandra is great, but I'm going to give her a lower performance rating than I gave John because while they behave exactly the same way with clients, she's a woman and shouldn't act like that at work." Right? Sounds ridiculous.

And yet, in study after study, we see that subconscious cultural and societal influences on our brains lead us to exactly those outcomes. And it's not until we examine those outcomes—or have someone point them out to us—that we realize we're getting them repeatedly. More on my experience with that later.

Now, most of this book is about conscious behavior and how to leverage it to both prevent building the type of organization you don't want and support building the type of organization you do. But in many ways, since the vast majority (around 99 percent, according to scientists) of things our brains process are handled automatically by our subconscious, like the examples above, it's incredibly important to talk about how these biases affect every one of us and therefore every organization in which we work. It's so important, in fact, that Facebook open-sourced the training that I helped create on this topic so that other people and organizations could use it for their own purposes—either to deliver as-is or to use as seed material for their own programs, discussion groups, etc. You can find the materials and take the class yourself here: **managingbias.fb.com**

BEING A PART OF THE PROBLEM

I generally assume that most people are good, despite what sometimes seems like an overwhelming amount of evidence that they're not. I certainly assume that *I* am a good person the vast majority of the time. So the first time I met with Sheryl Sandberg to talk about creating a training program about unconscious biases for Facebook employees, I was incredibly curious as to how we were going to position the training. I assumed, I believe correctly, that most of the people who would take the training were like me: they were good people who were just as stymied by the existence of harmful bias as the people who were the unfortunate recipients of its negative impacts.

It was at this point that I learned the first valuable lesson about bias that I encourage you to consider, especially if you're even remotely tempted to think: "I'm not part of the problem."

Not being a part of the problem is not the same as being a part of the solution. To a woman and/or a person of color who has been harmed by the presence of harmful bias, it's cold comfort to hear from a "good person" like me that I'd never consciously do anything to hold them back, because my unchecked unconscious can and often does do that for me. Even when I desperately want it not to. By not knowing what my unconscious biases were and how they might affect me and my decisions, I was a part of the problem.

And, as we see in many organizations filled with people like me and, probably, you—specifically, people who believe that they too are innocent of any contribution to the problem of harmful biases—as soon as they think they are "beyond" it, they start generating bad results. Results like uneven representation of men and women in leadership roles. Low—sometimes shockingly so—representation in a company's employee population from underrepresented minority groups. Not calling out behaviors that hold women or minorities back from making their full contributions at work, or not allowing them to be their true selves.

From a learning and development perspective, examining your biases only requires a couple of things from you in order to be a meaningful exercise. First, you need to admit that you're a human being. No, really, that's all you have to do to get started here, because all human beings have biases. If you can admit that you're human, the whole "having biases" thing is a condition of your humanity. That simple admission leads to the second requirement: you need to be open to understanding all the things that your unconscious brain likes to do with information while you and your conscious brain are focusing on living your life. As I mentioned earlier, science has shown that around

99 percent of the things our brain processes it does without our conscious involvement.

I'll stop there in case you need a moment with this (as I did—it's incredibly difficult to admit that we control so little, especially if you're a bit of a type-A control freak as I am). If you're fighting this notion of unconscious activity, consider this: How much conscious thought are you putting into how your shirt or sweater feels on your left shoulder blade at this very moment? How heavy your watch feels on your wrist? How much light is in the room, or how the paper of this book feels against your left thumb?

Come on, be honest: you weren't consciously thinking about any of those things—if you were, you'd be unable to concentrate on reading because your brain is a shitty multitasker.

But here's the thing—your brain was taking in all of that information, because it all factors into how you respond to the world around you and, when necessary, how you make conscious decisions about what to do when either your brain doesn't like the status quo (e.g. this sweater itches my left shoulder blade, so I'm going to go put something else on instead).

Let's look at this a bit differently—think of the last time you met someone for the very first time. After saying hello or shaking hands, did you say—out loud or to yourself—"Hey, new person! Give me about thirty seconds so I can form a first impression of you before we get to talking!" Of course not—but your brain did start forming that first impression unconsciously.

And what was it based on? Most likely nothing to do with the person and everything to do with you. Your brain immediately started considering things like what the person was wearing, how old or young they were, if they looked or sounded or acted like anyone you'd previously known, etc.

If that new person you met was similar to other people you'd known and liked, trusted, or respected, there is a greater likelihood that you were prone to liking, trusting, or respecting the new person. Because our conscious and unconscious brains share one big thing in common—they crave efficiency. It's much less work for our brains to process the familiar than the unfamiliar, after all.

TESTING YOUR UNCONSCIOUS ASSOCIATIONS

This might all sound very theoretical, and you're right—one of the most powerful things you can do to understand what the hell your brain is doing without your conscious involvement is to test it. For that, I'm going to highly recommend that you put down this book and get yourself in front of a computer to take a couple of the incredibly interesting and admittedly imperfect Implicit Association Tests (IAT) at **https://implicit.harvard.edu**. You can pick from any number of topics, but since so much of what we're talking about in this book is work- or career-related, I highly recommend the Gender-Career and Gender-Science tests.

Go ahead, we've got time!

Now, before you think that you're a terrible person—a

common knee-jerk reaction to the test results that reflect things that we don't like—there are a few things I've counseled myself and lots of other people over the years that I'd encourage you to keep in mind:

1. These tests measure implicit or unconscious associations. They do not measure bias in behavior.

2. The tests are not perfect. Years of teaching the content to engineers reminded me of that, and they're right. But the tests are helpful in starting some deep reflection or some valuable and meaningful conversations.

3. The point of taking the tests is to raise awareness, not issue verdicts.

So why do the tests? From an educational perspective, I use them not to sum you up but to open your mind a bit. In the classroom, they're intended to jumpstart the conversation about what people's brains do unconsciously that might surprise them. Me? I wasn't just surprised by my results. I was floored by them.

Why? I started off my journey into my unconscious associations by taking the Gender-Work IAT. I figured if anyone would have at worst a neutral association between work and gender and perhaps even a slight association with men being at home and women being at work, it would be me. My mom went back to work when I was in kindergarten and continued to work part-time well after my dad retired. I majored in communications and HR and organization development in college and grad school, respectively, and then spent much of my career in learning and other HR roles—fields dominated by women. My entire reporting chain at Facebook was made of strong women whom I valued and respected, all the way up to Sheryl, who reported to Mark.

So imagine my surprise when I learned that not only did I have implicit associations between men and work and women and home, but they were strong ones. My unconscious had betrayed me.

I definitely did not have a burning desire to disclose these results. I was embarrassed by them and horrified that it had likely colored my decision-making over the years when managing and working with women at school and at work. It was Sheryl who set me straight—"You live in the world. You're not impervious to movies and TV and books and everything else in the culture that you've experienced in a lifetime. The tests aren't verdicts; they're tools to help you think differently about how you think."

That consolation and guidance shaped how I eventually taught the class to thousands of people all over the United States. Still, it wasn't always easy, especially because the test results painted a clear picture in which men, specifically white men, usually came out on top. And I say that as a white man myself.

The classroom in which I taught this content became a classroom in which *I* learned, too. In the very first activity, we showed a quick video clip where five different people—all of whom worked at Facebook at the time—introduced themselves by saying, "Hi, I'm [name]—nice to meet you." I asked people to do what I'd never ask them to do in real life—make a snap decision about which of those five people they'd bring in for an informational interview about working at Facebook based just on that introduction. They didn't want to do it—and yet, when I reassured them that they were already all employed and that the exercise was only meant as a tool to better understand first impressions, boy, did they do the exercise.

Some people, I found, had incredibly active imaginations. They loved one person's perceived friendliness but thought another was standoffish. They thought some people dressed like engineers and therefore tended to like them more; they thought one person was great for going to Cal Tech. It should be noted that, if you watch the video, you'll see that the guy *is* wearing a Cal hat, but as a frequent wearer of baseball hats myself, I reminded them that wearing a Cal hat didn't mean he attended school there, just like I hadn't gotten my degree at Nike. We all laughed, but the moment stuck—if they made up such intricate impressions about how a person was or wasn't a team player or whether they were a "fit" for something based on just a few words and seconds, how might they be doing it in the real world with even more data and even higher stakes?

In discussing that activity, we talked about what I mentioned earlier—nobody meets someone for the first time and then says, "Hey, give me a minute to form a first impression of you!" It just happens. It happens in interviews, in client meetings, in social settings. It happens all the time. And it matters because people who we like for whatever reason don't have to work as hard to get "in" with us, and people who we don't like for whatever reason do. Our unconscious associations and biases, and the stereotypes that form about others from those things, often issue verdicts on others without our knowledge and without that other person getting the chance to be liked or disliked for their acts instead of their identities.

I and the people in the classes I taught often took comfort from a quote from Jesse Jackson we featured early in the class—"There is nothing more painful to me at this stage in my life than to walk down the street and hear footsteps . . . then turn around and see somebody white and feel relieved." Even a civil rights leader had bias—bias that affected how he viewed and felt about people of his own race.

I also learned that the more comfortable I got in talking about my own biases, the more comfortable everyone around me seemed to feel too. I told the story about how one of my female employees at Facebook had had the courage to confront me about decisions I had been making about who on our team was attending/speaking at conferences. She felt like she wasn't being included in those opportunities and rightfully wanted to know why.

As soon as I started saying the sentence out loud, I knew that I had been a perpetrator not just of holding a bias but acting on it. I cringed as I said the words, "I didn't want to ask you to leave your kids to go to . . ." I couldn't even finish the sentence. We both knew that I was an imperfect manager before that moment, but without training, the experience of the IAT, and the significant amount of soul-searching I'd done, I would have had to rely on her to point out the error of my ways instead of realizing it myself.

(And, FWIW, she reminded me that any opportunity to get a break from being a mom and go to Vegas to speak at a conference was a welcome one and that she would make those decisions for herself, thankyouverymuch).

So why am I including a chapter on bias in a book about owning your role in a company's culture? Simple: the research shows unequivocally that companies that believe they are meritocratic—distributing individual and collective rewards purely as a result of effort, not at all attributable to biases—often have the worst outcomes. And you can't have an organization with a winning culture if you don't acknowledge the fact that all companies are filled with humans and all humans have bias. If you don't create an environment where people can own those biases and have the language to call them out when it matters most (hiring, performance reviews, feedback, etc.), you can't build an awesome company.

If you are a manager, this means that without awareness and an environment in which people feel comfortable calling out bias, you are more likely to hire less diverse candidates, and, when managing people, treat whites and men with greater favor than women and/or people of color. Especially women with children at home.

If you are not a manager, the risk is still high with you, too, since nonmanagers still do incredibly important things like interview candidates, give peer feedback in performance review processes, and, of course, interact with their coworkers all day, every day. Being aware of your biases helps you control them, or at least correct for them, when doing these critical tasks.

How you get started is critical, so here are some other things you can do to get a better grasp on how your unconscious biases affect you:

1. **As with so many other parts of this book, you will make significant personal improvement if you can commit to becoming a better scientist of your own behavior.**

   Remember earlier when we were talking about how nobody stops themselves after meeting someone new to form a first impression? That doesn't mean you can't do it—you just have to be willing to examine your reactions consciously. So the next time you meet someone for the first time, ask yourself, *Why did I like or not like that person? Am I being fair? Is it about them or about me?* These questions won't erase bias, but they'll make it a lot more likely for you to better understand why you react the way you do to new people.

2. **Be willing to talk openly about the things that you're learning about yourself when in behavioral scientist mode.**

When I get in front of a room full of smart people and tell them that their brains often betray them, they don't always want to hear it. It's hard to admit that good people could ever require a black applicant for a job to possess eight more years of experience than his white counterpart just to get an interview, but the data is clear: they regularly do. Or that men *and women* are more likely to dislike women who are assertive and successful, yet more likely to like men who possess the same characteristics. But I do admit just that—without being diligent about my own behavior and my responses to others, I am at risk of submitting to my lifetime of exposure to stereotypes about women and men and minorities. I don't want to do that.

3. **Encourage people around you to explain their thinking when you have reason to believe that bias may be present in their decision-making.**

I do *not* encourage you to whip out your index finger, point it at a coworker, and yell "You are being biased!" But one of the luxuries that comes with being willing to talk about your own attitudes, beliefs, and biases is that it will more often than not create an environment where others will join you in doing so. And by asking questions instead of making accusations, you and they can learn more about why they think the way they do. So if you think that someone might be exhibiting an unconscious bias about how women are expected to behave (nice, accommodating, putting others first, etc.), you can ask things like, "I want to be fair and consistent here, and I think John behaves the same way we're describing Jane's behavior—are we holding them accountable to the same standards?"

4. **You can absolutely recommend training on this incredibly important topic.**

Biases don't want to give up their hold on our brains easily—they have to do so much less work when they're on autopilot, after all. This desire to do less work will manifest itself in some pushback. People will not want to admit that their brain does anything without their express permission, especially things that might make them look like bad human beings. Don't run from these conversations; run toward them. You cannot fix a problem that you cannot talk about, and while I initially hesitated to engage when things got heated in my classes, I learned over time that those passionate exchanges were often where the most learning took place.

I'm still not perfect at this and likely never will be, and I still hate that my associations about gender, race, and work aren't what I'd like them to be, but I know them now, so they have less power over me and my behavior. You can achieve that, too.

MIRROR MOMENTS

1. What have I learned about my biases that can help me

spot them more readily and counteract them when they pop up?

2. What will I need to do to continue to build my skill and confidence in identifying the impacts of bias not only on my behavior but also on the behavior of others?

3. What conversations might I need to have and with whom about how this has affected me or our organization in the past, and what we can learn from it?

MOVE TO ACTION MOMENTS

- I'm a straight, white man and the current system works just fine for me. I'm not doing anything that I'd describe as actively contributing to holding others back.

- Someone called me out once for appearing to be biased, and I got really defensive and denied it in the moment, but when I honestly thought about it, they were right. It hasn't come up again, but I know it's still "out there."

- I'm a woman who has purposely described other women's behaviors in ways that reinforce stereotypes and perpetuate biases. I've called their behavior aggressive or bitchy because I know that doing so will make it harder for them to get ahead.

BUT WHAT ABOUT . . . !?

I took some of the bias training you suggested, and I'm fairly shocked at the results. I've been at my company for a long time, and I am worried my subconscious has really affected my work and relationships here. What should I do?

Like I said earlier, being willing to be open and human about this goes a *long* way. If, as you examine your own biases and behaviors, you determine that you have said or done things in the past that might have limited other people, the first and most important thing you can do is commit to stopping that from happening in the future. Only you know for sure if it's going to be useful or harmful to address actual past behaviors, but if you do think it will be valuable, you can always point to newly acquired knowledge and growth as the reason for your change in behavior. "I was reflecting about how bias affects us all, and I want to be sure that I'm being consistent and fair, but I'm not sure I have always measured up to that standard."

I want to have some conversations with my coworkers about the results of their bias training so we can talk through how to be better as a team. Is that OK? Or are other people's biases none of my business?

Other people's biases are for sure your business, especially because those biases affect our collective performance, but as I said earlier, you have to be human about it. Assume that the person is unaware of their behavior and is therefore also unaware of the bias that is leading to that behavior; use questions instead of statements to make the point if you think they'll take the feedback defensively. There's a big difference between saying, "You're being biased against women!" and, "We need to be consistent about holding both men and women to this standard, and I think we might be heavier-handed when assessing women."

12 | The Chapter about Failing Harder

If you haven't figured it out yet, it bears repeating: 99 percent of the time, the thing holding you back from greatness is fear. Fear of what people will think of you, fear of the unknown, fear of being vulnerable. I would love to tell you that overcoming that fear means you are going to succeed. That's certainly what TV shows and movies would like us to believe. When you take the risk and do the thing, success is yours. Wouldn't that be nice?

But what about what happens when you're standing on the other side of a project and it has failed? There's no sugarcoating it, no two ways about it. The project—the thing—has failed, despite all your best efforts.

Now what?

There are plenty of TED talks and feel-good stories of self-made people who have failed and are now billionaires as a result of that failure. Those stories are great, but they're not what this chapter is about. No matter what your job title and no matter how organized you think you are, failure is as much a part of life as success is. It's maybe even more important than success.

But the truth is, we are not hardwired to accept this. We tend to think of failure only as the cost. Money, productivity, time, reputation. We aren't hardwired to think, "What can I learn from this, and how can I grow as a result?"

The good news is that you should know by this point in the book that I believe strongly that we are all capable of changing our bad habits into good ones. We are also capable of turning our failures into growth. You are going to fail sometimes. Embrace that as fact, and be the type of person who can look to that failure as a step toward positive growth.

A CONTROLLED EXPERIMENT

In the early years at Facebook, it was kind of a weird badge of honor for interns to do something that took the site down. Why? Well, if someone figured out a way to take the site down, that meant that they had probably found a vulnerability that could compromise Facebook unexpectedly. By breaking it ourselves, we could not only proactively fix that glitch but also make it so that particular situation would be much less likely to happen in "production."

Now, of course, Facebook has teams of people whose sole purpose is to keep Facebook up and running, but think about the value that type of activity might have in your own work or personal life. If you can figure out how to prevent a failure from happening, you are proactively solving a crisis. And a crisis averted is the best type of crisis.

For a long time, Facebook had internal mantras, memorialized in posters that live on the walls of offices around the world, that greeted employees daily: "Fail Harder. Fail Faster." This type of aggressive beta testing is something that sets

Facebook apart as a large technology employer. I have seen so many technology companies over the years refuse to release a product or service until they see it as "perfect," so they pilot *ad nauseam*. Not only is all this hesitation emotionally exhausting, but it also misses a seriously important point of risk-taking: there will be parts of projects or initiatives that will fail, and you will have to learn from those mistakes and fix them later. Waiting for a perfect product is waiting for something that doesn't exist.

This is not to say that you, your team, or your family should throw out all reasoning and just say, "Fuck it!" the next time you have a big decision to make. Another of Facebook's mantras, "Move fast and break things," isn't meant to be taken literally. Hardly. What it does mean is that when you take a risk, you are doing so with your eyes completely open to the possibility of both success and failure.

I've worked with many teams over the years, but you don't need to have a role like mine to see companies and teams that are really great at running their own controlled experiments. I recently went to a taping of the TV show *Will & Grace*. (If you haven't been to a taping of a TV show before, might I suggest making a field trip to LA sometime soon?) The twenty-two minutes of the finished half-hour sitcom you see on TV take hours and hours of work and countless people to make happen.

This is what I witnessed: A show like *Will & Grace* doesn't win tons of comedy Emmys for itself and its actors by accident.

The team knows what success looks like (and, based on the audience's laughter or lack thereof, what it sounds like), and they are working toward that as a common goal. That work means running a scene, carefully gauging the audience's reaction to the scene, and then making necessary changes to meet their goal more effectively the next time.

Over and over again, until they get it right. There are a few things that stood out for me at that taping that I will never forget when working on iterative work with a team of people:

- It's highly unlikely that your first pass is going to be your best work, so if you go into something expecting it to fail (where "failure" means it's not yet your best work), it feels less daunting—expected, actually—when you don't get it right.

- If you set aside your ego and focus on getting the best idea out there, even if it's not *your* idea, you will generate better work. More brains equal a higher chance of success.

- If everyone trusts not only the process but also each other, you can worry less about not hurting feelings and instead optimize for getting the best outcome.

There were several scenes where the audience *was* laughing, hysterically too, and yet the writers and actors weren't happy enough with the outcome—they still rewrote. And then the final product was *still funnier*, even though the audience thought the original version was . . . funny enough.

But if you're an Emmy-winning TV comedy, funny enough doesn't cut it. So a fourth item is in order:

- ○ Listen to feedback from others, but also listen to your own expertise, especially when you're at risk of settling for "good enough" so as to not avoid failure.

And that is what I mean by using your role as the conductor of (or at least a portion of) a controlled experiment. Try something, be focused on the outcome of that something, and when something doesn't work, fix it.

Over and over again. Until you get it right.

THIS IS NOW YOUR RISK

There is a great anecdote that makes its way around management circles about a man who failed big-time at his job. A million bucks lost, public embarrassment . . . that kind of failure. The story goes that when he was called into his boss's office the following week, he was expecting to be fired for his mistake.

"Fire you?" his boss replied. "No way. We just invested a million dollars in your training."

OK—I generally hate anecdotes like this because they're simple and feel bullshit-y. You're like, "OK, but who was the person and the company? This sounds too good to be true."

If you're thinking that way, I agree. But the moral of the story still applies. Specifically: many companies espouse the virtues of innovation, risk taking, and even failure, and yet very few actually understand what that means. Good managers don't encourage failure, they encourage people to be *OK* with failure. They recognize people who make informed decisions as leaders, and they particularly recognize people who learn from their mistakes and grow as a result.

Of course, being averse to risk boils down to fear. When I started at Facebook, I had the annoying and Stockholm syndrome-y habit of always seeking approval from my manager, always checking with him to make sure I was doing the right things.

"Let me give you some broad parameters," he told me. "If what you're doing falls within those parameters, you don't have to ask. I will have your back." This was his nice way of telling me he didn't have time to hold my hand while I did my job.

And what happened as a result? Instead of spending a bunch of time second-guessing, I pushed forward. The self-imposed obstacle of approval-seeking was gone, and I was able to take risks and really affect change.

To be clear, I did fail. Big-time. In the fall of my first year at Facebook, I thought it would be a great idea to launch a marketing campaign to coincide with the launch of a bunch of new learning programs at the company. I had my team create really slick posters ("GET YOUR LEARN ON!") announcing a learning month. I had table tents (the things you see at restaurants that have the day's specials on them, for example) listing the calendar of activities and courses that were coming. And I had T-shirts made.

Oh God, the T-shirts.

See, we thought it would be cool to put the infinity sign on a shirt with the word "growth" underneath it in order to get people to think of learning as an infinite process, with the classes we were launching serving as the core of that journey. We ordered around fifteen hundred shirts and shipped them to all of our offices. We put the posters up all over the place. We put the table tents on every table in every cafe in Palo Alto.

Sounds fine, right?

OK, so you know how a train wreck or a car accident seems to happen horrifically and in slow motion?

First, everyone hated the posters. While they would have looked great at any of my previous, larger, and more established employers, Facebook was still really unlike most other big companies. People had a lot of sensitivity (and I knew better) to how things looked—if graphics looked too "corporate," they were rebuffed. Our posters looked *really* corporate. Strike one.

Second, several of our senior leaders hated the table tents. "What the fuck is all of this shit in the cafes? Is this a learning team or a diner?" Strike two.

And then the shirts.

If you're a woman or have ever met a woman, imagine where (a) the infinity sign is going to land on her and (b) where the word "growth" is going to end up. Then imagine me in the fetal position on the floor lamenting the end of my career.

OK, stop laughing. Seriously. It was *so unbearable at the time.*

But I stayed six more years after that, so the rather visible and massive failure didn't end my career at Facebook.

I recovered. I apologized to the people who were upset about the look and feel of it, and they accepted my apology. Women everywhere forgave me while also steadfastly and often hilariously refusing to ever put on the T-shirt. We took the posters down and the table tents went away. I even apologized to Mark a few days later (this all went down on a Friday, so the weekend after was *super* fun for me and my team) and he, despite all my worrying and fretting, really didn't seem to have any idea what the hell I was talking about. In the grand scheme of things, there was something about my personal epic failure that, in all my inward-looking angst, I had forgotten:

It didn't matter.

Facebook wasn't a poster-making company. A marketing campaign gone wrong wasn't going to do a damn thing to hurt the company. I wasn't the most important employee at Facebook and my work wasn't the most important work.

Failure feels really big to us when we experience it, but unless you're seriously lighting the place on fire or doing something really bad, it disappears to others while it lingers for us.

Don't let it linger.

OK, back to business. (SERIOUSLY, STOP LAUGHING AT THE SHIRT!)

When it comes to failure, your role is important to understand both in terms of what failure could mean and how broadly it might ripple out. If you tend to be the sole decision-maker on your team, your risk of failure might feel greater as the buck stops with you. If you are part of a huge, well-managed team, you might feel the safety that comes in numbers when you are working on a new project or initiative. The more isolated you are in your role—the more public, indeed, the more creative the risk—the bigger opportunity for failure.

And as with everything in life, when it comes to risk you will need to assess your tolerance for failure. Obviously, you will not be able to see the future of any decision you make, from getting in the car to drive to work in the morning to investing a huge budget into a new program for your company. But that doesn't mean you shouldn't do it.

Again, I'm not saying every risk should be taken. But J.K. Rowling, in one of the most impactful commencement addresses I've ever heard in my life, shared this perspective with the 2008 graduating class at Harvard: "It is impossible to live without failing at something, unless you live so cautiously that you might as well not have lived at all—in which case, you fail by default."

Preach, J.K.

REFLECTION

How important is reflection in any role? In life? Very, very, very fucking important.

If you're not reflecting, you're going from uncontrolled experiment to uncontrolled experiment.

The *Will & Grace* team have their way of doing things. Facebook engineers have their way of doing things. That won't be yours, your family's, your team's. But you can replicate some of what you see other people doing well. Maybe you can get more feedback. Maybe you can create your own "studio audience" in the workplace. There are plenty of ways you can replicate the good parts you see in any process, adapting them so they work for you.

Wouldn't it be great if I could end this chapter with some sort of worksheet that will allow you to know—without a doubt—whether or not your risk is worth taking, and whether or not failure awaits?

I can. In fact, you've been doing this, too, probably since the first grade.

PRO	CON

Yes, the trusty pro-and-con chart. My advice is not to get hung up on the specifics. Be detailed in your overall assessment of pros and cons; share with people who know and love and want the best for you; and take any and all constructive feedback.

Then take the risk. Or don't take the risk.

And understand that failure is a natural component of both of those decisions.

MIRROR MOMENTS

1. What opportunities have you passed on taking because of the chance that you might fail?

2. How have you managed your work or the work of teams you belong to so conservatively that you've prevented failure but also stymied innovation and creativity?

3. How have you handled failure badly in the past in an attempt to make it look like (a) you didn't really fail or (b) the failure was someone or something else's fault?

MOVE TO ACTION MOMENTS

◦ You just completely fucked up a project. Badly. It's not the end of the world in any sense, but it *is* the end of that project.

◦ You're leading a project on process improvement and you're making small, incremental bits of progress, but people *including you* aren't pushing themselves hard enough. You're not delivering enough progress to justify the amount of time it's taking.

○ You took an informed risk and it paid off, but others around you are focusing more on what could have gone wrong than what actually went right.

BUT WHAT ABOUT . . . !?

How do I translate this into my personal life?

Great question—first, failure and fucking up don't really care whether you're experiencing them at home, the office, school, church, or wherever. While it's true that the stakes can feel higher at work because our ability to earn a living may be at stake, most failures at work aren't that serious, since we don't get fired for most of them. Similarly, the vast majority of our personal failures don't ruin our personal lives. I think the principles at play here—perspective, and being more curious about what you can learn from the failure than luxuriating in the delicious misery of having experienced it—are just as valuable if you want to move on from them.

For example: I set a personal goal in December 2017 to walk 525,600 steps that month. It was an homage to the song "Seasons of Love" from the Broadway musical *Rent*—there are 525,600 minutes in a year, so I thought it would be a fun challenge.

I am an idiot. It was a huge commitment—16,955 steps

per day, which for me translates to just over eight miles every day. In December. In Chicago.

I'd committed the cardinal sin of posting publicly on Facebook that I was doing this because I thought the public pressure would egg me on. It did. But when I got to the fifth day, I felt like hammered shit and only managed to walk just over 10,000 steps. My inner "OMG I AM A FAILURE" dialogue started.

I publicly committed! I made a big deal about it! I told EVERYONE about my goal! The wave of drama washed over me like the cold front that was sweeping the Midwest.

And then it stopped. It didn't stop because I hadn't failed to hit my goal, it stopped because I went into scientist mode instead. I quickly asked myself, "What do I need to do to recover? How do I prevent *one day* falling short from ruining an entire goal for a whole month?"

So the next day I walked more, and a few other days I walked more, and in the end, I *surpassed* my goal. By keeping the failure in perspective and refusing to let failing one day turn into failing for thirty-one, I made failure help me do better—not *feel* better about doing *worse*.

How do I help other people on my team both recognize and even reward failure?

The best and most obvious way is to talk about your own failures. Talk about the fact that you've *survived* them, and then talk about what you learned.

Look, we all experience failure, and when we do, it's pretty likely that others are going to see it. Admitting that you failed, and others admitting that *they* failed, doesn't make the failure real—the failure itself does that. What it *does* do is create an acknowledgement of reality that forms a space where we can analyze our failure, be human about it, and maybe even partner on ideas about how to do better the next time.

As with most things in this book, why not go first? Propose a "Let's talk about some things we screwed up and what we learned from them so that we can all help each other get better" conversation, and then be willing to take point. I've seen this done in many team and organizational settings, and the people who propose it have never looked small for doing so—quite the opposite. (Re-read the sentence above about most failure being well-known, whether we talk about it or not.) I can't say that this won't feel a bit scary, but I can confidently say that unless the failure you're admitting to is lighting the building on fire, you'll likely start a wave of open conversation about the obvious, and look like and be a leader in the process.

13 | The Chapter about Being Happy and Fulfilled (vs. "Having It All")

We as a society talk about "having it all" all the time. But what does that even mean? A career? Friends? Family? Time to pursue "outside" interests once your responsibilities are met? I'm guessing many of this book's readers have all of these things, and yet they struggle every day with balancing them in a way that means having a fulfilling life.

This might be a hard chapter to read. It's certainly been a hard one for me to write, because despite years of effort and trial and error, I still haven't perfected it. And you might have a million knee-jerk reactions as to how the things we're going to talk about don't apply to you or how, for any number of reasons (I call 'em excuses), the life you have isn't your "fault."

If you are reading this chapter, some shit has happened to your life, and some of it probably needs some addressing, if not a complete overhaul. The point of this chapter isn't to fix *all* of life's challenges. It's to manage your behaviors and to build awareness about prioritization—how it has an immeasurable impact on your outcomes, and how those outcomes lead you either closer to fulfillment or further away.

In the chapter about strengths, we talked about the fact that you can't be good at doing *anything* you set your mind to.

We should also talk about destroying the gigantic lie that it's possible to have it "all" (absolutely everything you want or think you want), because that's exactly what it is. A gigantic lie.

I've seen people at every company I've ever worked at or with struggle with the topic of work-life balance, for example. I've been one of them myself. All of these organizations have employees—in some cases, tens of thousands of employees— who seem to think there's a secret formula to working eighty hours a week and raising a family and having hobbies and doing enough for others and . . . if they could just figure out *the secret to having it all*, they'd be masters of the universe, able to do it all flawlessly.

I've seen myself and many of my peers struggle when we think that we're failing ourselves, our companies, or the people who matter most to us when we aren't able to juggle the bazillion demands that modern life can place on us. And, of course, I've seen the massive amount of self-induced pity that can come from the constant comparison of the realities of your life to what are oftentimes the highlight reels of their own lives that others share on social media.

None of this leads to a good place if the outcome you desire most is to be happy and fulfilled. Happiness and fulfillment, in my experience, are more closely associated not with having it "all" but with knowing what you truly value, knowing what you truly do *not* value, and then prioritizing accordingly.

RISK/REWARD OR COST/BENEFIT

When I took the job at Facebook I did so knowing that leaving my home city of Chicago was going to be the hardest thing that I'd have to do. I'd spent my entire life searching for the city that helped me feel at home the way that Chicago did, and I knew that San Francisco didn't have the same effect. Nevertheless, the opportunity was in San Francisco, so back to the Bay Area I went.

I legit cried for most of the drive from Chicago to California. I knew that I was making a huge trade-off of personal happiness for professional opportunity, and even though I'd made and accepted the decision—and really positively anticipated the work opportunities and challenges that lay ahead for me—it still hurt. But by the time I got there, I resolved to speak fondly of Chicago when asked but also avoid thinking or speaking bitterly about San Francisco. I *mostly* succeeded.

At about the three-and-a-half-year mark, however, the trade-off felt too big not just *some* of the time, but *all* of the time. As much as I understood friends and colleagues who genuinely loved San Francisco, I couldn't bring myself to feel the same way. And while I loved my job, and probably gave twice as much to it as I would have if I'd lived in a city I really liked, the weight of not being happy outside of work crept in more frequently. I felt it was posing a very real risk to my performance *inside* of work.

I definitely didn't want to quit my job, but something

needed to change, and that something was the place that I lived. So I transferred to Facebook's NYC office, where I then spent an incredibly rewarding year and a half helping to build our staff from a couple hundred to a couple thousand people. I reconnected with my love of theater and got involved in many cultural experiences outside of work that fulfilled me in ways work could not. For the first time in several years, I made friends who weren't coworkers and had very different lives and jobs than me, people who didn't care to know the details of my daily work life (nor I theirs) and just wanted to be friends. I was happy.

At the same time, making that move also put a bit of a damper on my career prospects. I had done the reverse of what most people in many companies do—I'd moved away from the center of the company, not toward it. While there are any number of roles that could or even should be played away from a company's HQ, mine wasn't really one of them. In moving away, I accepted that doing so would probably result in a slow-down of my career growth trajectory.

This doesn't mean that I didn't work as hard. It doesn't mean that I blamed anyone or any type of system for holding me back. I had simply made a choice to trade off a bit of career satisfaction and growth for a whole lot of nonwork happiness, and it's a decision I would make again and again. It's also one that I'm incredibly grateful to my leadership team at Facebook for supporting, even if they didn't always understand it.

One of the things that continued to stymie me, however,

was the number of people who either vigorously stated opinions about how I was throwing something away or swore that they would never make a similar type of trade-off because of what others might think of them for doing so, what they might be "giving up" (the dreaded FOMO). It's as though they believed that accepting a high degree of personal unhappiness—whatever its source—was a reasonable price to pay for professional success.

I was in no position to judge, as I had, after all, made those same arguments for years. But I got to the point where I decided that having it all meant something very different than I'd thought before, and I was ready to make some significant changes to how I lived my life in and outside of work.

This all, of course, leads to a larger point: I couldn't have had the HQ-centric career in NYC and ultimately back home in Chicago without an incredible amount of personal sacrifice in the form of long nights, working late, and lots of cross-country travel. Sacrifice that could have and likely would have caused myself and those around me a fair amount of harm. Instead, I had a very honest conversation with myself about what I actually valued, what would really bring me happiness and fulfillment—the elusive "all"—and then got about the business of making it happen.

PRIORITIZING: WHAT IT'S ALL ABOUT

Once I got to NYC, it was like the universe was conspiring with me to weave this newfound ability to focus on what mattered most to me into the work I did in the classroom. I had the opportunity to operationalize this prioritization exercise in a program that the head of global sales at Facebook, Carolyn Everson, commissioned the learning team to build, for which I will be eternally grateful. Carolyn is incredibly passionate about people leading personally meaningful, fulfilling lives—especially in the face of incredibly high demands, ambitions, and stakes—but the specifics of what that meant and required would take some focused work.

I'm going to walk you through one of the activities we built into that program now, as I think it will help you (as it helped me) hone in on what *really* matters to you based on what you actually *do*, not on what you *say*.

First, list all your major priorities, whether or not you're giving them the time and attention they need and deserve. Then add to that list any other things that are taking up reasonable amounts of your time. It's not yet important to do anything with the list other than generate it.

Once you have come up with these items, put one on each line under a column in a simple spreadsheet (example below) and label that first column **Activity**. Note that these activities need not be ranked, just present. Once you've listed them all, assign the following values to them in adjacent columns:

- ○ **Importance** refers to how important or not this activity really is to you on a scale of 1–10. Again, don't rank compared to other items on the list of activities, just say how important/worth your time it is.

- ◦ **Current Priority** refers to how much or little prioritization (e.g. time spent doing it) this activity gets. Again, 1 means next to none and 10 means the maximum amount. Do not rank or order them compared to others.

- ◦ **Gap** refers to the difference between the importance and the priority. If you said something was a 10 for importance but a 2 for priority, you have a gap of 8—you're saying it's important to you but admitting you're not giving it much priority. (Lots of people put going to the gym here!) If you said it was a 2 for importance but a 10 for priority, you still have gap of 8—no negative numbers. It just indicates that you're saying it's not important but acting like it is.

- ◦ **Acceptable to me?** asks you if the gap is something you can happily live with. Is it OK that you really want to be in better shape (exercise as an activity has a high "importance" number) but aren't making the time to exercise (because it has a low "current priority" number)? Maybe, maybe not. We're not here to judge, we're here to help you judge.

- ◦ **Acceptable to others?** asks you if the gap is OK for the people in your life who are impacted by it. For example, if you've said that family is of high importance but getting little prioritization, I can almost assure you that the people in your family aren't cool with it. Note: a guess is fine for the sake of this activity, but in the grand scheme of things you shouldn't just guess if the gap is OK for others—you should ask them to know for sure.

○ **Actions to take?** is where the rubber meets the road—specifically, it asks you to identify what things you should be doing or not doing to close the gap between what you say you value and what your actions *show* you value.

Note: This is never static. It is changing all the time. Every single day you will be confronted with changes, choices, and things that are beyond your control—indeed, most of what happens in the world is beyond *anyone's* control. Maybe it's the guy who brings donuts into work on the second day of your diet. Maybe it's the unexpected injury of a spouse. Life can and will happen, and there will always be circumstances that are beyond our total control. This chart isn't concerned, per se, with those outside forces and whether or not you can control them—it's concerned with how you respond to (read: prioritize) them and whether the things you *can* control (read: your choices) are working or not.

It's not a matter of taking those priorities away. It's a matter of managing your reactions to them and then prioritizing your behavior accordingly.

Priorities	Importance [1-10]	Current Priority [1-10]	Gap	Acceptable to me? [Y/N]	Acceptable to others? [Y/N]	Actions to take:
Physical condition	8	2	6	N	Y	Shift morning meetings to later in the day to allow for workout time
Family commit-ments	3	8	5	N	Y	Get help for Mom and Dad around the house

When all is said and done, you're almost surely going to have some gaps. When I went through this exercise, what I found was that I was regularly putting everyone and everything else in front of some of the basic needs I had for my own well-being. Specifically, I was working too much, exercising too little, and spending too much time on the road for work. I had to be really honest about the fact that while I was reaping incredible rewards and building great relationships at *work*, my *personal* life was suffering, my physical health was deteriorating, and—hardest of all—I was experiencing those negative outcomes because of choices I was making and consequences I was ignoring so I could have it "all."

Ultimately, I had to make some important decisions about what I did and didn't want, and then had to accept that those decisions (a) were going to require trade-offs and (b) would have very real impacts on the people around me.

And so do we all.

There are other things to consider here, too. Obviously not everything can be a 10 in terms of importance. Not everything can be your top priority. Once you've gone through and identified your priorities, ranking them is a good second-step activity. It can also result in some really good conversations.

For example—lots of people make their first year at a new job a huge priority, oftentimes making personal interests, family, and friends a lower priority until they feel established and confident in their work. Sadly, most of us don't talk about this type of prioritization with the people who are affected by these choices, so our relationships unnecessarily suffer as a result. Imagine how much easier it would be for you (in the form of less guilt and angst) and the people you love (in the form of feeling less undervalued) if, instead of just hoping for them to figure out on their own that your work is taking a temporary front seat, you actually said, "Hey, you are incredibly important to me, but this new job means so much to my career and to me. In the short-term I'm probably going to prioritize work over my personal life and people like you, but know that I value you, too, and I hope you'll give me the feedback if I make work too big of a priority."

One sentence to avoid so much drama! And I know what you're thinking. You're thinking, *Who talks like this!?* And the answer is, in fairness, hardly anyone. But I'd argue that's why most people struggle unnecessarily rather than successfully preempting or better managing the conflicts that their choices can bring about.

You might also realize that you're prioritizing something that doesn't deserve it. Lots of people—myself included—tend to put the needs of others first. This is a noble thing to do, but like anything, it has its limits. If you are finding that a lot of your time and energy are dedicated primarily to doing things for other people, you run the risk of generosity fatigue and your own well-being taking a nosedive. It's important to do things for others, but it's also important to take care of yourself. And it's *very* important to avoid doing things for others who only take and never give in return.

THE BALANCE WILL ALWAYS SHIFT

It's also worth noting that this isn't an exercise that is performed once, solves all the conflicts about time and effort in your life, and then is done forever.

For example—when I revisited my chart about a year after moving to NYC, something was still not "right" for me. I was still doing really well at work, I was involved in a ton of things outside my career, but I had become *more* busy. Some of the busyness at work was replaced with busyness in my personal life because I hadn't yet learned how to manage a lower intensity setting—at all. I was organizing huge events to get people interested in the theater, raising hundreds of thousands of dollars to support the #EduHam program that helped so many high school students learn about the founding era of the United States and gave them a chance to see *Hamilton: An American Musical* in cities all over the country. I was *busy*. And while I loved what I was doing, I was quickly burning out.

The company around me had changed too. It had gone from constantly building and testing new things to scaling those built things up to thousands of people. Being much more of a builder than a scaler, the work had become less fulfilling to me. My priorities had shifted.

So I made some of the hardest and scariest decisions I'd ever made about my career—I moved back to Chicago full-time and started rebuilding the personal life I'd put on hold. I left an incredibly rewarding role at Facebook. I started my own consultancy, Multiple Hats Management. I wrote this book. I dropped what we mostly lovingly referred to as the Facebook fifteen—though it was probably closer to twenty. I reassessed my priorities and made some hard choices to make the life I was living more like the life I knew I wanted.

Your balance will shift, too. There are lots of things that change what we care about as time goes on—we get serious about relationships with other people. We maybe even marry them! We adopt pets, we start families, we move to new cities. We take on new and unexpected responsibilities when our kids, friends, or other family members need us to help them carry burdens that weren't anticipated. Loved ones get sick.

The lists are as endless as the variables that affect our lives. The only things we can *really* do if we want to be the owners of our happiness and fulfillment revolve around constantly and *consciously* prioritizing and reprioritizing while being honest with ourselves and others about the trade-offs that accompany the decisions we make about how we spend our time and energy.

PROACTIVE/REACTIVE CONVERSATIONS ABOUT TRADE-OFFS

I mentioned earlier an example of talking to friends or family members about prioritization in the first year of a new job. There are lots of other conversations that you can have *proactively* about these types of trade-offs to mitigate the negative side effects that your prioritization might have. Or to help others help *you* realize the positives that can come with getting your priorities in balance.

- Talking to your team about how becoming a new parent is going to impact your work schedule and prioritization once the child is born

- Talking to your manager about what matters most to you (refer back to the chapter on building great management—this is the first item on that list) and where you want or need to make changes to bring those priorities into alignment with your daily life

○ Talking to people who can help you out when a shift in your activities (e.g. leaving a job that allows for limited flexibility in schedule to take a lower-paying but higher-fulfillment job that does) negatively impacts your income

The common thread here is *talking about it*. Without these conversations, we leave too much up to chance—others magically figuring out what matters to us, what drives us, why we behave the way we do, etc. You and I both face the chance that someone we confide in or need help from will betray us, tell us "No!", or even get in the way of us achieving our goals, but you will *for sure* stay stuck in your current circumstances if you don't prioritize and identify how others can help you achieve the things that matter most to you.

HAVING IT ALL MEANS BEING OK WITH NOT HAVING IT ALL

Ultimately, you are the best judge of what matters to you. You are also the person to praise if your life is in alignment with your priorities and the number-one culprit if it is not. Others can contribute to or detract from your happiness and fulfillment, but only if you let them and only if you are unclear about what you value and what you don't value.

And while people may think you are a bit weird for bucking tradition or going against the norm, they will also think you're pretty amazing if you are genuinely happy regardless.

MIRROR MOMENTS

1. What trade-offs have you made that have impacted your happiness in a negative way, and why did you make them?

2. What conversations have you either not had at all or had reactively about the impacts of your priorities, decisions, and behaviors on other people?

3. What benefits are you realizing from living some or many parts of your life in ways that contradict what you say *really* matters to you (e.g. "I'm miserable but I'm making a *lot* of money!" or "I stay out late having a lot of fun during the week and am tired all the time at work, so I am regularly passed over for more challenging or rewarding work").

MOVE TO ACTION MOMENTS

○ An opportunity to go out to a long dinner with friends comes up, but would require you skipping the gym for a third day in a row.

○ You've taken a role that ends up taking far more time away from your friends and family (long work hours, frequent multi-night travel away from home, etc.) and your relationship of six months is falling apart.

○ Your son wants to add a fourth after-school activity to his busy roster of hobbies; the only way you can accommodate it is to give up a weekly lunch with a close friend you otherwise rarely see.

BUT WHAT ABOUT . . . ?!

OK, this is great, but I have kids. How does this apply to me?

You have kids, someone else has reserve military duty, someone else has sick parents to care for—the list goes on. I don't mean to undervalue or underestimate the requirements that accompany the role of parenting, but I also resist putting more moral value on one person's priorities and decisions about what matters to them than I would on those of another who chooses differently. We all have things that matter to us, we all have others depending on us in some way or another, and we all have to own how we meet the many obligations we face.

That said—since I don't have kids of my own, I would imagine that being a parent makes this *more* applicable, not less. Prioritization is hard enough when the needs you have to worry about the most are your own; those needs are compounded when they involve other people.

This is where doing the prioritization activity from this chapter *as a family* or with your partner can really help you have serious conversations about how everyone has some *personal* priorities and some *shared* priorities and how there isn't limitless time or energy available to do everything. It's not fair to expect children to just figure out how their interests or needs impact other people—siblings, parents, etc. Helping kids understand how they fit into the bigger picture and how they help shape that bigger picture through their own behavior is an important parenting moment, and activities like this can help you and them better communicate about why and how you decide to spend your individual and collective time.

My partner/kids don't understand the devotion to my work life. How do I fix this?

First and foremost, why do you think that is? Have you actually *explained* why your devotion to your work means so much to you, or have you just expected that they will understand that it matters to you because you spend so much time doing it? That they should, therefore, just . . . figure it out? In so many cases (between managers and employees, between friends, and between spouses) where there is a disconnect, there's at least a conversation or two that didn't happen, often because it was assumed that everyone was on the same page by . . . some other means than direct conversation.

It's also important to remember that by making the choice to be in a relationship or have kids, you've created a responsibility to prioritize them. They might *fully* understand your devotion to your work life but also fully *not* understand why that means you are always putting work first. This is where, again, having open and honest conversations not just about what matters to you but also *what matters to them* is important if you're going to have any chance of meeting all of the various needs. And you have to keep that channel of communication open because . . . things shift and change.

But I did all this stuff, and my perfectly laid-out plans were messed up. Now what?

Even the *wording* of this question implies a lack of ownership. "My plans were messed up—now what?" is a passive way of explaining a crappy outcome. "I thought I had planned really well but I didn't anticipate *this*—now what?" is better.

That said—the most important first step you can take when a plan fails is to be honest about why and how you got the results you got (e.g. I said losing weight was a huge priority but I didn't exercise enough or stop eating junk food all day). There will always be extenuating circumstances that are beyond your total control—like the fact that junk food exists in the first place, or that your coworker Joe is always testing out cookie recipes in his spare time and bringing the delicious experiments into the office to share with his coworkers . . . including you, and you're on a diet!

I'd also question the notion of "perfect" plans. If you think your plans are "perfect" then you're probably overly confident about the plan itself going off without a hitch and less focused on the execution of that plan—*especially* when there *is* a hitch.

And there almost always is at least one. It might be a "perfect" plan to say that you're only going to eat 1,200 calories a day on your diet, but it's a flawed plan if it doesn't also account for how you're going to deal with tempting baked goods from Joe. Or the fact that your partner is someone who can eat anything at all without gaining weight and regularly does so. In front of you. In front of you and your kale salad.

Look, if your plans mess up, the first and best place to look is *why* they messed up—what you either didn't anticipate or didn't know how to manage when it appeared—and then go back to your plan and make it better, smarter, or more realistic.

14 | The Chapter about Getting the Hell out of Your Own Way

"Our deepest fear is not that we are inadequate. Our deepest fear is that we are powerful beyond measure."

—Marianne Williamson

Before you do any of the work that the rest of this book implores you to do as you face the various inflection points in your career, you must do *this* work in *this* chapter. The good news is that the work in this chapter is fairly simple. It doesn't vary from person to person. It's a universal truth. You are extraordinarily powerful. The actions you take or *don't* take every single day are the most important determining factor in your successes and your failures, both personally and professionally. There is no one in the world who owes you anything, and there is no event, situation, boss, unlucky break, or celestial alignment that is more powerful than how you react to situations in determining your destiny.

Great, right?

Well, yes and no. It's great because it's incredibly liberating to realize just how powerful you are in determining your fate.

It's also downright scary. Because when we really start

examining our patterns, a lot of us are pretty shitty about taking control of our own lives. We blame others for our problems. We get caught up in bitchy gossip that only makes bad situations worse. We see ourselves as the stars of our own lives but see other people as the directors.

Those habits are hard to break. But the work you put in toward breaking bad habits with regards to ownership is probably the most valuable work you will ever do in terms of your career and your personal life.

It's worth it.

PATTERNS, PATTERNS, PATTERNS

I often talk about the importance of people becoming scientists of their own behavior. If you missed it earlier, what I mean is taking a serious step back and examining yourself in the same way a scientist would: without emotion or judgement. Not because emotions don't matter or because how you feel is irrelevant; quite the opposite, actually. Emotions drive a lot of our behavior and they're incredibly influential in our lives. But they're not particularly useful when objectivity is required, and lots of objectivity is required when analyzing behaviors. Especially when those behaviors and behavioral patterns are your own.

So, since we already have our lab coats on anyway, let's start with a little science. I did my masters thesis on something called *locus of control*. Simply put, this psychological term describes how a person sees themselves in relation to the world around them. People with an internal locus of control tend to see themselves as actors *and* directors. They see themselves in control, and believe that the events in their lives are unfolding because of decisions and actions they make. People with an external locus of control see life as happening *to* them. They are constantly blindsided by obstacles and see themselves as victims of happenstance. They are acting out scenes that someone else is directing.

You can probably guess which type of person I am, and which type of person I am drawn to.

There is an incredible amount of upside and, I think, a minimal amount of downside to having an internal locus of control. I can't think of a single great leader I've worked with who didn't have an internal locus of control. Happy people, I think, are far more likely to have an internal locus of control, because they do things actively to make their happiness more likely. When they are unhappy—and they definitely experience unhappiness, just as everyone does—they see themselves as the first and most important resource in addressing what's wrong.

Simply put, people with an internal locus of control see themselves as players in the great game of life. People with an external locus of control see themselves as passive subjects and, often, victims of it.

This is not to say that people with an internal locus of control see themselves as the *only* player in their destiny. Certainly, there are millions of ways you have been fortunate (or unfortunate) in life. You have had lucky and unlucky breaks along the way. Having an internal locus, or seeing yourself as a player and not a subject/victim, is not the same as seeing yourself as some sort of godlike superhuman. You're not.

So why do we do this? Why do people who are generally smart and capable fall into the bad habits of seeing themselves as victims and sabotaging their own careers and relationships?

Because while it can feel amazing to be the person who solves all the problems, has all the answers, and sees their role in everything that happens to them, it can *also* be deeply satisfying for everything else to be someone else's fault! Things being the fault of someone else makes it easier for us to feel good about not doing anything to solve our problems. I don't know about you, but there are a *lot* of problems in the world today that I don't want to own or accept any responsibility for creating or perpetuating.

But tempting as it is to smugly point the finger of blame, I also want these problems to cease to exist, and so I force myself back into the director's chair and get to work. And, when it comes time to *act* in ways that will get me closer to that result, I put on that hat, too.

Having an internal locus really means that you see yourself primarily as the sum of your behaviors or patterns of behavior. You can tell me a million times that you are an easygoing, laid-back person, but that doesn't make it true. What makes it true is when you act that way. Most days, if not every day. Your everyday patterns and behaviors *are* who you are. The way you handle small and large stresses and events in your life sets the stage for your experience.

In other words, if you want to be known as a certain type of person, you have to *be* that person, *especially* when it matters most. You have to be in control of yourself and your shared experiences.

And the work starts by simply paying attention.

YOU ARE NOT A VICTIM OF YOUR LIFE

Look, I get it. It's often *really* hard to break old habits. It takes courage and skill to call out crappy behavior, whether it be yours or someone else. No one wakes up and says, "Hey . . . how can I be a victim today?"

The next time someone you know is being helpless and super victim-y about a problem, do something simple but provocative: ask them, "Are you actually enjoying telling yourself that you have no ability to prevent or solve this problem?" They might get really pissed. OK, they'll *probably* get really pissed. They might want to punch you in the face. They might storm off and ignore you for weeks on end. But they might also, on some level or another, see what you're calling out—that by seeing themselves as powerless, they're making themselves so. And, more importantly, even if they don't want to see it, others see it bright as day.

So if you see yourself as someone who might have the tendency to play the victim as opposed to taking control of your destiny, don't worry. **You can change.**

Any teacher can tell you that their role comes in two parts: technical and emotional. This book is going to go through a lot of "technical" aspects of being, cultivating, and maintaining an awesome attitude, which contributes to an awesome work culture. But it is true that none of those things will make a difference without getting into some difficult and often emotional stuff. We aren't robots, and everything we do is going to be influenced by the personal joys and setbacks we face as human beings.

Simply put, a healthy work culture starts with healthy work humans. That's what I want you all to be, no matter what your role or level or tenure or profession is.

Let me start off by saying that in all my years as a trainer, an HR professional, a "camp counselor," and—my most important role—a human being, I have heard and used every excuse in the book when it comes to why people are unhappy. I'm too *this*, I'm not enough *that*, my boss does *this*, my coworkers do *that*. My spouse, my family, my house, my dog.

On and on.

I'm going to say something really important here, and I'm not going to sugarcoat it. We have all been through some tough shit. I say that sincerely. Hardship and setbacks don't give a quarter of a crap how much money you have, where you come from, who you know, what resources you have. There isn't a single person who hasn't had their share of tough times. You have, I have, and every person you encounter has. Tough times are part of life.

There's a lot of stuff in life that you can't control. But the way you react to those things—*that* is what is going to define you, not that they happened in the first place. And the ability to see yourself as or transform yourself into someone who has the same ability to put themselves into as many positions of ownership and accountability as are humanly possible is not a skillset that is limited to any one group. We all have that ability, and we can all use it.

But before we dive too deep into the large obstacles of life, let's take this everyday scenario: you are ten minutes late for a meeting. Which of these responses best describes your handling of said scenario?

a) Gah, I'm sorry I'm late! There was traffic as usual, and then this guy cut me off right as I was trying to turn into the parking lot. Can you believe that? I was so rattled I had to pull over for a second. Then, of course, I spilled my coffee walking down the hallway—thankfully it was no longer hot, but can you imagine if it had been? Ugh, so anyway, it's just so frustrating. I just need a do-over for today! Actually, for the whole week! Who is with me??
b) I'm sorry I'm late. What did I miss?

Let's be clear. This is the same situation here. The same person, even. The first version of you rattled off excuses, made the interruption to the meeting even longer and *more* distracting, and, most importantly, showed yourself to be unaccountable for your own lateness.

Being late happens to all of us. It's usually not a big deal, usually something you could prevent if it's a habitual thing, and usually nothing that requires a lengthy explanation. No one cares why you were late. The people in that meeting might have been sitting in the same damn traffic jam; they'd just left their houses twenty minutes earlier. Or didn't stop at Starbucks on the way despite time being tight.

They just want you to sit down and get on with it.

The smallness of this issue isn't the problem. It's the *mindset* that is cancerous. Because when the stakes are low and you don't take responsibility, what will you do when the stakes are high?

As you will see over and over in this book, the people I've encountered who are the most successful in their work and in their lives are the ones who take accountability for their actions. Accountability does not mean listing off excuses for why things aren't done. It means making the changes you need to make to fulfill your commitments. ("Hey everyone, because the traffic is so bad in the mornings and I have to get my kids to daycare, I won't be able to get to the office before nine thirty for our weekly staff meeting. Can we schedule the meetings at nine thirty from now on? If not, I'm happy to call in.")

For some of you, this type of accountability is scary. You want to be seen as flexible, committed to your role, perfect in every way. Well, you're not perfect. I've spent a lot of time in this book asking you to make peace with your imperfections. And I'm telling you that this type of accountability—honesty—is what your bosses and coworkers will appreciate and admire in you.

They'll also reward behaviors they see in you that model accountability. Every time you position yourself as a player—in control—of your life and your reactions to experiences, you will be proving yourself as someone who is worth taking a risk on, worth promoting, and worth investing time and energy in.

YOU ARE [PROBABLY] YOUR OWN WORST ENEMY

You don't need to work at Facebook to know that any social media platform can be a hotbed for victim behavior. Tell me if this post looks familiar:

If social media has done anything, it has proven that we are indeed our own favorite subjects. This isn't new, but it's never been this on-display for so many people. Don't get me wrong— plenty of good comes from social media, and that will be the topic for another book. But anyone with common sense knows that Facebook can be either the highlight reel of our lives (think about those perfect selfies we see all the time, not the ninety-nine attempts that were . . . less perfect) or a place for people in a victim-spiral to find company in their misery.

The person who posts things like what I've posted here is rarely asking for help. He is not generally concerned with solving any problem. He is certainly not contributing to anything substantial. He's looking for reinforcement of his victim-hood. He's hungering for some likes and some comments from friends along the lines of:

"Life is SO unfair to you!"

"You just have to suck it up and hope that someone will stop ignoring your awesomeness at some other point in time!"

"This happened to me too! #FML!"

Calling this type of behavior out publicly is tough but possible, and you absolutely should do it. But calling it out privately can be a lot easier.

Let's go back to that traffic obstacle we just talked about. Why would I bring up traffic twice in one chapter? Because I absolutely hate driving, and I especially hate driving in traffic. I remember one time when I lived in California, I came in hot after a ragey morning behind the wheel and spent the first five minutes of a meeting railing about stupid drivers, traffic, and all the ways life sucks because of automobiles.

"So, is this going to get any different or better in the coming years?" someone asked me.

"No," I answered. Of course not. Traffic gets worse, not

better, especially in the Bay Area.

"Then you should probably come up with a different way of coping with it."

Of course, my initial response was, "Hey! Screw you! I'm the one suffering here!" I guess I had some rage leftovers.But then I realized what this person was actually trying to tell me. My behavior was unhealthy, was never going to make the situation better. The only person suffering was me, and I was doing so *by my own hand* . . .

Words matter. Your words set the stage for your actions, and your actions define who you are. Do "players" deal with traffic? An annoying coworker? A difficult project? A challenging interaction? Of course they do. You probably just don't see it because they're too busy solving the problem to either complain about it or bother with anything that will waste their time.

We all need to find healthy ways of dealing with *all* obstacles, both personal and professional. And you have a choice to be a victim or a player.

So, let's do some role-play.

Obstacle	Victim mentality (do not recommend!)	Player mentality (highly recommended!)
Traffic	Bitch and moan. Refuse to make adjustments to time and schedule.	Change your meeting times and shut up about it already!
Being "overwhelmed" by a project	Bitch without solutions. Gossip about all the ways this project is "impossible." Make it seem as though you are the only person with that problem. Get no results.	Ask what you can do to change your behavior and get different results. Do what you can with what you have. Get unstuck.
Not getting promoted	"I was passed over." "I was not #blessed." Go on social media to complain and ask for approval and reinforcement of victimhood.	"I haven't earned this promotion yet." Be vocal with the decision makers, explaining why, seeking feedback.

If you are a manager, who do you want to promote? The truth is, we are entertained by people who bitch and complain, but we are drawn to and respect, promote, and advance people who *get shit done*.

That is what I mean about being your own worst enemy. Your reactions to the challenges you face are the most important determining factor in your successfully navigating them, not the obstacles themselves.

I still don't like driving. I just don't. But I also choose not to make it worse by reacting in unhealthy ways to the *many* frustrations that driving brings. You can choose this, too. And the more you choose it, the better you will become at it.

The truth is, our reactions to challenges in our lives are choices. Are some challenges harder than others? Of course. Is it totally appropriate to take an afternoon and scream at a wall? Sure, I guess. If it makes you feel better. I doubt it will help you *do* better.

But also know that if you are reading this, you have gotten through 100 percent of the challenges you've faced in your life. That's right. You have a perfect record of getting through hard shit, as evidenced by the fact that you're still here to tell the tale. But I want you to get through hard shit faster and with less emotional drag, for you and for the people around you.

And you always have a choice. Always. That is the empowering part of all of this.

KNOW WHEN TO ASK FOR HELP

Despite all this internal power I have hopefully helped you realize within yourself, don't make the mistake of thinking you are somehow invincible. Or perfect. In fact, getting over this need for perfection might be one of the biggest obstacles of all to overcome.

Just because you see yourself driving your own proverbial car doesn't mean you won't have mishaps along the way. In the same way you'd change a tire when it gets flat, you'll need to ask for help, often, from people who know more than you. That is great. Ask for help, and give help away freely.

All that is part of the process of getting out of your own way on the path to success.

MIRROR MOMENTS

1. What are some of the things that happen in your life where you occasionally or routinely play the helpless victim?

2. What impact does your refusal to take ownership of some of the unsuccessful or counterproductive behaviors you use have on you? On others?

3. Where have you let obstacles win instead of finding ways (on your own or with the help of others) to work around those obstacles?

MOVE TO ACTION MOMENTS

- You interviewed for a new role that you felt you were perfect for, but another candidate got it.

- One of the people you work with is a total asshole to you and her behavior is affecting your desire and ability to get your work done.

- You really hate your desk location because it's near a "gathering spot" for people to stop and chat, making it really hard for you to focus and get work done.

BUT WHAT ABOUT . . . !?

How do you deal with a person who is stuck in victim mentality, but can't seem to see themselves that way?

I tend to follow the three-strikes rule. Specifically, I will point out three different examples of where I see them doing something that is perpetuating the victim mentality. The first example will be the softest ("Have you considered what role you might be playing here?"), the second a little less so ("From what you're describing, it sounds like you're contributing [x] to the problem and therefore the inability to move past it"), the last and final one the hardest ("I don't think I'm going to be able to help you here. The feedback I've given you about your role doesn't appear to be sinking in or impacting your behavior"). I do not feel bad about walking away from people who don't want to help themselves, especially after repeated attempts to help them see a path forward.

When is a challenge "too much"?

I'm not sure I've ever encountered a challenge that was too much, per se, only challenges that were maybe too much for me to do without help. Generally, I find that the more up-front I am about my limits and where I think I'll be at capacity and need help, the less likely I am to surprise others when I come asking for that help. And the less daunting it is to ask for it at all—after all, I am only behaving in a way that being up-front already told you I would!

What happens when you try to fix a major obstacle in your job, only to be told by management that your suggestions can't be done?

I don't believe in picking your battles, because it implies that something worthy of being labeled a "battle" is something you should ever walk away from in the first place. That said, I have had plenty of experiences where I felt that I was right and that my leaders were wrong. Earlier in my career, I got super idealistic and probably a bit insufferable about it. What I have learned since is as follows:

I rarely have all of the information that others have, so I should never assume that I do. Given this, if I want to better understand why I'm not getting my way, it's probably better not to try to convince others why I'm right but rather to ask them why I'm wrong.

Given the above, I also don't assume that the people I'm trying to convince understand or see the problem the same way that I do, so I make sure to empathize with that lack of context and work to help them understand why I feel or think the way I do.

If, with all the understanding in the world, we still don't agree that what I'm proposing is the right thing, I either have to rage quit (not recommended!) or acknowledge that if there's only one problem for me to solve, I'm dangerously unvaluable and therefore have bigger things to worry about; if there are *more* than one problem for me to solve (much more likely), I should probably go tackle those instead of investing more time and energy (mental, emotional, and otherwise) into a dead end.

15 | The Chapter about Leaving Well

There is a common misconception that, when a successful, privately held company goes public, everyone working there is an overnight millionaire. At least, that was my experience at Facebook. The morning after the Facebook IPO, a woman in line behind me at Starbucks noticed that I was wearing a Facebook T-shirt. Despite my strong intuition to not engage in conversation, I mistakenly made eye contact, and the door was opened. She excitedly asked if I worked at Facebook, and when I acknowledged that I did, she asked me *with zero shits given about the inappropriateness of it*, "How are you going to spend your millions!?"

I was shocked by the directness of the question but somehow had the presence of mind to say, "Well, the first three dollars are going to this Americano. The rest we'll wait and see."

Most other assumption-laden questions were about turnover. Everyone assumed that there would be some sort of mass exodus, and anyone who'd gotten on the Facebook train early was now purchasing their own private island to retire to immediately.

Of course, that is not reality. After Facebook went public, I remember being in a Q and A session with a senior leader who was asked by a nervous employee about the risk of high turn-over. "Aren't you worried about people leaving?" they asked.

The answer has always stuck with me: No. Of course not. In fact, the leader asked us to raise our hands if this was our very first job. So few hands went up that it was almost comical. People quit jobs—it happens all the time, for all kinds of reasons. The leader then asked everyone in the room to stop worrying about who was staying, who was going, and basically anything else beyond our control, and to instead stay focused on being great contributors now.

But for some reason, we as a society have such a dubious relationship with change. We fear it, we project our own insecurities about it, we talk about it incessantly, but we too rarely take steps *toward* it. Despite lots of pretty posters and mugs and slogans that remind us that change is the only constant, both personally and professionally, getting our relationship with it right can be incredibly and frustratingly elusive. This awesome job, even this awesome life that you have created, is fragile and inconsistent. This isn't something to fear, it's something to be empowered by.

The majority of this book has been spent asking you to be a scientist of your own behavior—to think about what you do and why you do it, so you can fix the things that need fixing and become a more impactful employee and human being. This work also relates to leaving a role at company. Yes, even leaving requires you to perform some self-reflection in order to do it well.

LEAVING WELL

When I was getting ready to leave Facebook and venture off into my new career as a self-employed writer, consultant, and owner of Multiple Hats Management, I knew that I wanted to model the idea of "leaving well." Not just as an insurance policy in the event that I wanted or needed Facebook to welcome me back with open arms should my newer ventures fail. I wanted to "leave well" because I wanted the way I left the company to reflect all of the great opportunities I was given while there, the people I met along the way, and the impact that the whole experience had on me.

This led me to reflect on people who, throughout the course of my career, had left their roles, teams, or companies with grace and good feelings. People who turned the sadness others felt about their departures into hope for their own futures and their own potential. What I discovered in the process was that the people I knew who "left well" all followed the same general rules:

1. They were humbled by their experiences. In each case, people who left well were the ones who were genuinely appreciative and grateful for the job that they were leaving behind, despite any ups and downs they surely faced. They were authentic in how they talked about their job, vocally proud of their contributions to the team or company, and aware that they were a part of something larger than themselves.

2. They clearly stated that they were pursuing something different, not better. They didn't talk about how much more exciting their new role was going to be, how much better an opportunity it was, how much it was going to finally bring them happiness, or, as we spoke about in the chapter about Organizational Stockholm Syndrome, how their new companies were going to be free of problems or cultural issues.

3. They were gracious in understanding impact. Losing a contributor can have effects that ripple across many employees and teams. Leaving well means being conscious of the impact, and making sure to set the future team up for success as much as you possibly can before walking out the door. It may also mean offering to be a resource after you leave.

4. They carefully cultivate relationships they want to continue pursuing. Leaving any role means an inevitable barrage of "Keep in touch!" and "This place just won't be the same without you!" People who leave well are the ones who give the team they're leaving the time to grow and adjust to their absence but are also willing to cultivate the lasting relationships they have made.

I know what you're thinking: *This is easy to do when you're leaving on your own terms. Plenty of us have been or know people who have been pushed out of a role or fired, and under those circumstances it's a whole lot harder to keep your head held high and focus on the positive.*

I would argue that no matter what the circumstances, these rules still apply. Maybe being humbled by your experience will mean being very clear about mistakes you made and things you would have done differently. What's wrong with being vocal about that? In case I need to remind you again, you are not perfect. None of us are. Own your contributions *and* your mistakes, and don't be afraid to share them with your new team or company.

I am hopeful that no one reading this book has had the experience of being a "rage quitter," but in case this needs to be said, *do not do that*. If there is a problem to be fixed, fix it. I've spent an entire book talking about how the company you work for is *your* company—however, no company is "screwed" without you, and no team is going to simply wither into oblivion without your expertise. In fact, if you see things this way, chances are you have been a large part of the problem, and you are doomed to make the same mistakes in your next role. (See again: Organizational Stockholm Syndrome.)

PROJECTING NEGATIVITY

I've left a lot of jobs in my life, and I've "started over" many times. I have found that when I tell people I'm leaving a place, team, or opportunity, I am greeted with a variation of one or two responses. Either people are thrilled for me and wish me well, or they project onto me their own fears and feelings about their own life choices.

I'll give you a good example. For just shy of four years, I worked at Intel, a company well known for the excellent perk of giving all of their employees a two-month paid sabbatical after every seven years of employment. Not only is this a great way to "force" people to take some much-deserved rest, it's a way for people to step in to cover these roles while an employee on sabbatical is out, which gives lots of employees the chance to expand their own experiences and opportunities.

When a friend of mine quit Intel to pursue a totally different career, she found that people either cheered her on or were obsessed with her sabbatical. For every "Good for you!" she was met with, "But you only have five years until your next sabbatical!"

It doesn't take a lot of work to see that the latter response is missing the point entirely. When someone tells you they are pursuing a new opportunity, they are not doing so in the hopes of getting your approval. At least, they aren't if they've read this book and are living an authentic life in the workplace. They are sharing a part of their lives with you, being vulnerable and likely an equal mix of excited and terrified.

If you are in a management role, this work of being self-aware in your responses to others is even more crucial. I'm sure you've figured it out by now, but it bears repeating since we so often forget the simple truth: happy and fulfilled employees make positive, successful contributors. Your job isn't to cling to your team with bloody fingernails and force them to stay with you. In fact, it can take months or years to recover from the impact of someone being there who doesn't want to be.

Your job is to create a relationship where you are celebrating your team's strengths and encouraging them to better themselves. Sometimes, that will mean letting them go to pursue new opportunities. In fact, if people want to leave, that probably means you've helped them realize their future potential. This is a good outcome of a job done well, something you as a manager should feel damn good about, and certainly something that the managers and leaders I worked with at Facebook should feel good about when it comes to me.

THE APATHY SPIRAL

It should be obvious by now that being successful in your roles, both personal and professional, requires having passion for the work. And while you might have every intention of keeping that level of energy with you every day, lots of things can happen over time to impact your passion. The company could go sideways. The economy could tank. The end goal for your project might shift and change, causing you to lose steam. Similarly, life outside of work happens. Babies are born, relationships change, and life events can shift your priorities.

These things happen. But you do not need to let apathy happen.

"Letting apathy happen" is one of the most insidious things that can happen to you, your team, and your company. Telling yourself that you "deserve" to stay in a role that no longer engages you because of the money and time already invested or because of the great impact you *used* to have is a recipe for disaster.

There's a great quote from Stephen Sondheim's *Sunday in the Park with George* about succeeding in the art world: "Even when you get some recognition, everything you do you still audition." While I used to think, *God, what a terrible environment to have to work in, constantly proving yourself despite everything you've already done*, I've switched perspectives. While I don't think it's anyone's responsibility to constantly have to re-prove themselves in basic ways to everyone else, I do think that the people who are constantly proving themselves *to* themselves and showing up to earn their place every single day have longer, better careers.

And it's OK to get to the point where you don't have that in you anymore. When Jerry Seinfeld ended his massively successful sitcom on May 14, 1998, he was considered a fool by many—he was at the top of his game, had the highest-rated sitcom on television, and was making millions and millions of dollars every week. NBC offered him more than five million dollars an episode to do one more season, but he was steadfast that he wanted to leave at that point, because there was nothing worse he could imagine than leaving his show with people saying that he should've ended it sooner. "Oh, yeah, *Seinfeld*. That show was funny two seasons ago," was his worst nightmare. And he wanted a life outside of his work, which he got. He didn't want to become apathetic about his work; when he felt that apathy coming, he walked away. I've never forgotten that lesson.

TAKE A LESSON FROM BROADWAY

Toward the end of my time at Facebook, I started venturing more and more into the theater world—certainly *going* to shows, but also dabbling in production. I got to know lots and lots of performers who live a life of performing eight shows a week, constantly auditioning, and keeping their eyes open for the next great role.

Over time I learned that if anyone is a model for leaving well, it's a Broadway performer. It's not a secret amongst Broadway performers that they're auditioning constantly—it's just normal. After all, you're likely going to run into people at these auditions that you're currently working with, and everyone on Broadway seems to have worked with everyone else on Broadway at least once, so there's no point in trying to hide it.

Change also comes at a breathless pace in the theater world. Shows that are going strong one minute can lose a star and close within weeks. Producers can decide at the last minute to pull funding, shelving a hotly anticipated show at a moment's notice. But performers don't stay away from Broadway because of the risk and the pace of change; they just consider it a normal part of doing business and act accordingly.

When one of my favorite theater friends, the Tony-, Emmy-, Grammy-winning actress Cynthia Erivo (of the musical *The Color Purple* fame) decided to leave the role and the show that made her a star at the age of twenty-nine, she made a few key points to me that I'll never forget. First and foremost, she would be forever grateful for the experience of doing *Purple* and for the accolades and opportunities that it brought to her. Not just in terms of other work but in terms of people, of experiences, and of memories that will stay with her always.

Second, she was also clear that doing a vocally and emotionally demanding show eight times a week for sixteen months and for a year prior to Broadway in London takes a toll. It also, as you can probably imagine, becomes somewhat routine, and a performer like Cynthia is committed to delivering the best performance every time they walk onstage because most of the people in the audience will only see the show once. That level of commitment is hard for even the best of us to sustain.

Finally—she believed in herself and her abilities enough to also believe that there would be other incredible opportunities out there that she might miss if she stayed in the relative comfort of a very successful show.

Symbolically, she decided to leave the show on her 30th birthday, and she did so with grace, with gratitude, and without regret. Like anyone leaving the security of a sure or a *mostly* sure thing to venture out into the great unknown, she had fears. But there were also possibilities, and those possibilities eclipsed the fears that came with jumping off into the unknown.

So on January 8, 2017, when she took her final bow in *Purple*, in front of over 1200 fans, she was saying a heartfelt goodbye to the thing that brought her so much fulfilment but that she was ready to let go. I saw it happen from the second row. The moment, and the courage and self-confidence that led to it, will stay with me always.

MIRROR MOMENTS

1. Think about previous roles that you have left. Would you say that you left them well? If not, why not?

2. If you've ever burned or even singed a bridge with a former employer, what benefits did that bring you and what consequences did you pay for doing so?

3. Think of someone you know who has "left well"—maybe even you. How did you view their leaving and what can you take from that example the next time you're ready to move on to a new role, team, or company?

MOVE TO ACTION MOMENTS

○ You've decided that your current role isn't challenging, and you've lost your passion for it. You're not sure if there's anything you can do to change your role, but you've not talked to anyone about that possibility, either.

○ You're for sure going to be leaving your job. The first person you confide in about your pending departure unleashes a torrent of complaining about their own role.

○ Your upcoming departure is going to have a significant

impact on the team you're leaving behind because it's right in the middle of a huge project and you are a key player on that project.

BUT WHAT ABOUT . . . ?!

I know that you said my team will be fine without me if I leave, but I do know it will cause a lot of difficulty for the people I work with, and I feel terrible about that. What should I do?

First, give yourself a little pat on the back for being concerned about the team you're leaving. I've found that in many cases, I continue to cross paths with people in multiple organizations, so I'm glad when we've been considerate of others as we move on.

The best thing you can do to honor that concern is to make sure you give notice that will allow you to set others up for success, document as much as you can about what you're working on, let as many people know as are affected by it, and then do everything you can up until your last minute at your current company to contribute to their success.

And by all means, offer yourself up to someone on the team as a resource after you leave if they really get stuck, need to ask you a question about something you may have missed on your way out, etc.

My coworker is constantly complaining about his role, and several of us have suggested he leave the company and start somewhere new to find happiness. He never does. How do we deal with the exhaustion of that?

Have you ever asked him why he's so unhappy? Have you ever highlighted to him the things you think he may be saying or doing to contribute unconsciously to that unhappiness? Have you actually been direct with him about the negative impact his attitude has on your team?

If there are several of you experiencing this, there are also several opportunities to address it head-on. ("Hey, Jack, we totally get that you are unhappy in this role, which can be really uncool to deal with, but we also feel that your unhappiness is affecting your work and our collective ability to get things done, and that's not cool either. We want to help you be happy in this role, but if it's not going to happen, you need to do something to either make things better or find a new job.") You may feel that your indirect (read: passive-aggressive) hints—your eye-rolling, your talking shit about his unhappiness behind his back, etc.—are the same or have the same impact as being direct, but they don't.

Ultimately, though, if you can do nothing else, remember that misery loves company. When misery comes in the form of Jack's unhappiness, don't invite misery into the room.

Afterword

We made it! And we covered a *lot*!

If you've read through every chapter, looked in *every* mirror and every moveable moment, and *still* feel like you have a loooong way to go, good! Nothing in this book is a quick fix, and life is a continuous classroom filled with opportunities to practice.

I've written in several chapters about how I still struggle with everything I wrote about . . . sometimes, *really* struggle. Fear? OMG, writing a book is one of the scariest things I've ever done. Not because writing itself is scary, but once it's out there, it's on my permanent record. I have undoubtedly said something or even *many* somethings the wrong way or made incorrect statements, and because it's committed to print, I can't go out and reclaim every copy of the book and fix the mistakes. They're just out there forever. And that's terrifying. So yeah, I still struggle with fear.

I have been fortunate in my career, though. I've deliberately surrounded myself with people who believe in me, who give me hard feedback, who encourage me when I need encouraging, and who bring me back down to earth when I get a little bit too far out there.

And I want to continue paying them back by continuing this conversation with you.

On Facebook.

At the time of this writing, over half a billion people use Facebook Groups every day to do everything from swapping Instant Pot recipes, to coping with the death of loved ones, to collecting stamps, and every other possible thing you can imagine that has at least two interested parties. I've set up a Facebook Group for anyone reading this book to join so that we can continue the work you've started in reading and that I've started by writing. (The address, again, is **www.facebook.com/ groups/thisisnowyourgroup**)

Maybe it will only be a handful of us and we'll get to know each other really well; maybe it'll become a huge community of thousands of people giving and sharing advice, best practices, tough love, and stories of successes and failures and second and third and fourth tries. I'm on board, either way.

As I mentioned at the beginning of all of this, about 90 percent of your learning and growth is going to happen from trial and error and support from others. This book was 10 percent—that group and your hard work will be the rest.

I hope you'll join.

Acknowledgments

To the people who have helped me get this book across the finish line: thank you. Brooks Scott, Aria Marinelli, Leah Wedul — my readers and givers of feedback and philosophical debaters I could not have done without.

To all of my colleagues at Facebook: I am incredibly grateful for the opportunities you gave me to learn and teach and fail and grow. To Stuart Crabb, the boss who hired me at Facebook, and Amy Hayes, the boss who made so much of the flexibility and freedom to do big work happen in my last three years, "thank you" doesn't seem enough. I wouldn't be where I am without you. Or without my other incredible past/current colleagues in Learning & Development at Facebook. FBL&D 4ever!

I am equally grateful for the road that led to Facebook, which was overflowing with experiences doing similar work with amazing people—my students and teachers and colleagues at Microsoft, Intel, and USAA.

To the people who have *really* taught me by letting me teach for them: Ken Blanchard, his life-changing program Situational Leadership II, and his incredible team; the wonderful people at VitalSmarts and, specifically, the authors of *Crucial Conversations* (Joseph Grenny, Kerry Patterson, Ron McMillan, and Al Switzler); and the people I consider to be the parents of the Strengths Movement, Marcus Buckingham and the incredible people at TMBC. Their ideas have profoundly influenced my life and everything I wrote in this book, and I am incredibly grateful for their continued partnership and leadership in so many ways. Please do yourself a favor and read *their* books, too.

But for *this book,* the biggest dose of gratitude goes to Roseanne Etcheber Cheng—not only for selling me on the idea of writing a book in the first place but also for putting her money where her mouth was and being an incredible writing coach, cheerleader, therapy-mate, and fellow *Hamilton* junkie. To the rest of the staff at Wise Ink, especially my diligent and resourceful project manager, Danielle Bylund, and the designer of the entire look and feel of the cover and interior of this book, Emily Rodvold: THANK YOU.

Finally—my sixth-grade teacher, George Bettinger, was the first person in my life to encourage me as a writer. Looking back on what I wrote in sixth grade is hard because almost everything I wrote was TERRIBLE. But it was clear to me and to him that I loved writing and that with work and dedication I could become good at it. People who see strength in us before we know what it is are worth everything, and he was the first person to not only believe in my potential but to encourage it. Thanks, Mr. B.